Finding Your Spouse, Getting Married, & Staying Married

GUIDELINES ON

BUILDING A CHRISTIAN HOME

ANDREW A. OMOTOSO

Living Fountain Publishing
Saugerties, NY 12477

Copyright © 2020 by Andrew Adebisi Omotoso

Living Fountain Publishing

Andrew Adebisi Omotoso
BA(London);
MA. Ed. D (Columbia);
M.Div. DMin (Nyack)
Emeritus Minister of Christian Education

Bethel Gospel Assembly
2-26 East 120th Street New
York, NY 10035

ISBN: 9798635355237

Printed in Manilla, Philippines

This little book is dedicated to my
current Grandchildren:
Similoluwa Teniola Olutayo
Oreoluwa Adunola Olutayo
Oluwakorede Olalekan Olutayo
Eva OlaOluwa Marshall
Christian IbukunOluwa Marshall
And the Others yet to arrive.
In the belief that they will find in these guidelines
Needed Help in intimately following
The Lord on the Journey of Life

Contents

Preface: Why This Essay?
Why Another Treatise on Marriage?

The decision to commence the writing of this piece of testimony was occasioned by a question my granddaughter Similoluwa Olutayo asked me in March 2019 in Coffs Harbor, Australia. The question was: "Grandpa where did you first meet Grandma?".

It is important to let it be known that SimilOluwa had just turned 15! So, I had to try to figure out what other questions queued behind that one single question and that those other questions would have to be dealt with and would not be satisfied with a short answer of "Yaba, in Lagos Nigeria."

I suppose those other questions would include something like: "how does one come to know whom to marry such that they can stay together long enough to become grandpa and grandma." Or perhaps is there a "right" way to know who would be your spouse and with whom you will live together with to become grandpa and grandma?

But there are other reasons for writing this book. The Lord had given us, my wife and I, a Ministry for the youth – The Encouragers Ministry. That Ministry, under the guidance of the Holy Spirit had reached out to the youth through weekend programs such as "Singles Retreat", "Married Couples Retreat" and a Youth Newsletter. These activities were suspended when the Lord asked us to go and serve in

Bethel Gospel Assembly Harlem New York in 2004. My granddaughter's question appeared to be a prompter that it was time to revive this Ministry and that this Testimony should be the way to resume this Ministry even as we were hearing the Holy Spirit nudging us in this direction.

Another reason for this book of testimony on Marriage is the need to show that in spite of the obvious confusion in the world today about what a family is, this record will be a veritable pointer to the Truth that God created family; it was not created by society, nor did it come in a kind of cultural evolutionary process. The family is the creation of God and He watches over what He has created and will protect and sustain all unions that follow His original design.

The fourth reason for this book of testimony is that I have come across a number of young ladies who, having waited over a lengthy period, to be asked for marriage, have almost given up. I write this book of testimony to encourage them not to give up. Their attitude appears to be that "if marriage will come, let it come, but if it will not, maybe it's not meant to happen and in any case I no longer care. I am going to develop myself to the maximum, enjoy myself to the full while serving the Lord in my calling." Those who adopt this reasoning are generally professionally successful young women who had earlier chosen not be involved in any serious relationship until they had become secure in their careers. There are also many men in this category, who wish to achieve their self-imposed levels of education and career and desired income brackets before even considering marriage. For this category of people, a wife or husband is another adornment on their list of accomplishments in life. Marriage is scheduled for when "they have made it".

There is yet another group, who having watched many marriages collapse all around them have come to believe that the emotional stress in marital relationship would not make the enterprise worth it for them. I was for a time in this category. ….

This attitude to marriage reminds me of a friend I had met in Ghana about 1960. A number of young men and women had gathered in the city of Sunyani in northern Ghana, to build an Incinerator for a local rural community. We had come through an international volunteer organization. He was from Canada. I had come from Nigeria. Most of us there, were youths who had just completed high school or were in their first or second year of college. When we departed after the summer program to our respective countries, some of us maintained correspondence with one another for a while. One day I got a rather strange letter from my Canadian friend saying among other things: "If this life has any meaning, I haven't seen it. So, I have decided to leave college, go to work, make money and then 'buy' myself a wife……" Those words have stuck with me these many years and I believe some of the singles reading this small book might be of that frame of mind, that a wife or husband is what you do when you have become "successful" in life. And of course, "success" is measured according to the definition of success in the world system.

You must probably have known marriages that were contracted just as an economic transaction in which each is severely committed to reaping from the relationship "what is in it for me". It is my prayer that some message here will show the meaning of the special relationship in love and marriage. No, a spouse is not just an extra adornment, a marriage is a necessary selflessness. Indeed, God views marriage as a sacred and highly exalted relationship!

Perhaps you might have been discouraged by the rate of infidelity in marriages that were based on an understanding from the beginning that the word "infidelity" would not exist in their relationship. Accordingly, I pray that as you read these pages, you would focus on Jesus Who is the Husband of the Church and Who has pointed us to what a true marriage means.

INTRODUCTION

Marriage was instituted by God. It was not a relationship that evolved from culture or was discovered by human society. God Himself created and ordained marriage. In Genesis 2:12 He declared that it was not good for man to be alone and created a help suitable for him. He did that after all other creatures had been created: birds of the air, creatures in the oceans and animals in the forests. Adam gave each of them a name. God declared that none of those would be a suitable companion for man. Then He created the woman from the man Genesis 2:21-24, and both became the first family on earth and were settled in the Garden of Eden.

We are the Masterpiece of The Self Existent Eternal Creator-God

The story of The Christian Faith originates as recorded in the Book of Genesis by the finger of God. No other story of creation has been able to bear the test of close scrutiny. We need to restate the basic Truths here:

God created the Universe by the Word of His Mouth as recorded in Genesis 1:1. He created the Universe out of nothing, ex nihilo. Some review of the story of creation is necessary here, because it is the foundation of the thesis being presented in this piece of work. It is a view that considers the Big Bang theory of pseudo-science as untenable. Here is why:

Everything that is, has a beginning. The computer on which I am typing this work has not always been, neither the table on which the computer is placed. Whatever has a beginning has a cause. The Computer was put together by a computer engineer. The Table was designed and manufactured by a furniture maker. So, when the computer was made, it began to exist just as the table on which it is placed began to exist upon its being made. And whoever and whatever caused the thing to be, had existed before the thing that was caused to be. Time for the item caused to be, begins with its existence and whatever causes the thing to be exists before and so is outside the time that marks the beginning of the existence of that created item which the maker caused to be.

So, whether you want to explain Creation as something that occurred as per the Big Bang theory, there was a time the world did not exist. Someone made the Big Bang happen after which the world began to exist. Whoever or whatever made the Big Bang is the cause and the Maker or Creator. Thus, the big Bang theory is not inconsistent with the Record in Genesis.

Now if you are one of those intellectuals who provide some other theory of Creation inconsistent with the Genesis Record, please spare some time to watch a movie called "God is NOT dead" based on a book by Rice Brooks or Read the book "Reasonable Faith" by William Lane Craig, for a more detailed explanation of the view of Creation as backed up by scientific reasoning.

However, it must be stated that this is not a book about Creation Story debate. This is simply to state that marriage was established at Creation; that it was not a thing that was initiated by man and it is being asserted here that there was a model of marriage that God the Creator established at Creation. This writing urges that this is the model to follow in order to reap the benefits that marriage was created for the first of which is procreation. Not only is this the model of marriage bound to succeed, because it is based on genuine love, it is quite doable. God says His burden is light and it is; it is the world's burden that is heavy. (Matthew 11: 28-30.)

The First Marriage and Humanity's First Parents

Thus, the first couple were blessed by God and empowered to flourish and replenish the earth. Genesis 1:28. Adam and Eve first had two children, Abel and Cane. The billions of people on earth today began with those two people Adam and Eve and then their children, Cain and Abel. Though there is no record that Abel had children, because his life was cut short by his brother Cain, God blessed Adam and Eve with Seith Genesis 4:25 and Noah came from the lineage of Seith. Okay you might ask "where did Abel, Cain and Seith find their wives? The answer is in Genesis 5:4. *"After he begot Seth, the days of Adam were eight hundred years; and he had sons and daughters"*. That is where their wives come from.

In Genesis 3:20, the Bible states:

"And Adam called his wife's name Eve, because she was the mother of all living."

Therefore, procreation by husband and wife is God's order of replenishing the earth. Accordingly let us establish the basic truths that govern the principles of marriage expressed in this book. The following are the basic beliefs which form the basis for this book of testimony:

The first is that marriage is between a man and a woman, from the beginning. It is the distinct truth that the world population is replenished through the union of man and woman Gen 1:27-28, who are husband and wife. That is Procreation. And as The Americans say, "if it aint broke these millions of years, why try to fix it?". But the Truth is, it can never be broken, because God is God forever. He is the unchanging changer.

Humanity Continues to Mar God's Plan with Divers Aberrations

Of course, man has interfered with many aspects of creation. Man has tried to alter what God created through all kinds of technical devices such as genetic engineering. The original nature of plants and animals have been tampered with and the food chain drastically interfered with, giving rise to dire consequences such as the emergence of hitherto unknown or rare diseases.

Man has similarly tampered with the natural process of pregnancy and childbirth. Some have decided that the only important thing about marriage is having a child and that science has solved that problem. You can buy an egg from a bank of unknown woman or buy sperm from an unknown man and get a baby, like a manufactured toy. You do not need a man or a woman to marry and live together to do that; so, marriage may not be that important in today's world. *The Midwich Cuckoos*, a science fiction, by Wyndham: Penguin Books: New York (1980) is fast becoming a reality today.

In that fiction, in the village of Midwich in England, a mysterious silver object appears in the atmosphere and the whole community fell unconscious. A day later, the object disappears and everyone recovers from their unconscious experience and resumed life normally.

However, every woman was found pregnant. The children born did not belong to their parents. They were all blondes with silver eyes. They grew up extremely fast and their minds were possessed with sterling abilities and exercised enormous control of others through those abilities. Similarly, George Orwell's fiction novel titled 1984, which is really no longer a fiction today as those technological feats described in that book written in 1949, are part of normal life experience today.

The rebellion, started in the Garden of Eden has continued to this day. Also, the consequences of disobedience as spelt out by the Creator in Deuteronomy 28:15-68, do follow. This rebellion does not change the Truth of creation and man rebels against the Truth at his own peril.

The second flows from the first, namely, that a purported marriage between a man and a man or between a woman and a woman, is an act of rebellion and an abomination. It is contrary to the pattern established by God and there are, as in the other cases of rebellion, evil consequences of previously unknown or rare diseases, social chaos and confused mind traceable to this particular act of rebellion. When rebellion has gone too far, God gives the serially disobedient up to reprobate mind. So, there are consequences for disobedience many of which are listed in Deuteronomy 28. These consequences will continue to unfold and there is final judgment in the offing.

A little departure from God is always a thin edge of the wedge. Little by little it expands until all generic sins become acceptable. The disobedient mind starts by giving a different name to things that God has named. Instead of its being called what it is, (abomination), homosexuality is being defined as "sexual orientation." (Romans 1:26-27.)

But how about Pedophilia? May we also call that a sexual orientation? What about bestiality? May God forbid us moving towards calling that also a sexual orientation. Forced underage marriage is made legal by some country's legal code. What shall we say about incest? Right now, in Northern Ireland, the Law Reform Commission is considering legalizing incest between consenting adults. May God forbid us descending into a complete state of confusion by renaming stealing and rape as say "mood orientation" or a kind of character orientation which should be permitted as we move towards a more "inclusive" society.

The word "inclusive" is being upgraded into the level of a moral imperative. The question is what makes "orientation" a permissible conduct that must be allowed in order for a community to be called an "inclusive" community? What would be a model "inclusive" community? Is it one in which like in Scheepers's *Hamlet Prince of Denmark*: "There is neither good nor bad, but thinking makes it so…" Act2 scene 2, a statement by someone getting out of his mind!

What makes an inclusive community good or better than a non-inclusive community? For instance, every religion is *exclusive*. In logic, 'to define is to negate'. Clubs, sororities are exclusive. Not everyone is a member. There are always exclusions of those who do not qualify or are not admissible. There is only one Faith that welcomes ALL without exclusion and it is not a religion; it is the Faith of Jesus Christ, the Faith of Christianity which is about *relationship*.

In any case what is necessarily "good" about the word "inclusive"? Is a community of Pirates or marauders "inclusive" and therefore good, by their admitting into their group murderers, thieves, liars, revelers, with equal rights etc.? Does the inclusiveness of an evil group make that group good? Or is there no longer 'good' or 'evil' but just a question of how one feels about it? The Bible speaks *"woe unto them who call good evil and evil good"*. (Isaiah 5:20). There are those who hold that there is no absolute Truth. If they hold that as Truth, then that also is not True, right, because how do they know that?

Thirdly, the definition of family is a man and his wife (a woman) and their children. That is one of the central beliefs upon which this book stands. I know that for purposes of government services a family is now being re-defined as a person and his or her *significant other*. In New York housing, that is how a family is defined in the application forms. There have been some bizarre developments from that kind of family definition.

Today the names of domestic animals are also being changed. Dogs, goats and other pets are now being called boys or girls depending on their sex and classified as members of the family on virtually equal basis with the children. This writer holds the view that domestic animals are pets and there is no reason to give them new names. A male dog is a dog and a female dog is a bitch; there is no reason to give them new names that make them indistinguishable from humans.

Fourth, this book is also addressed to those who don't know their identity or who may be confused about their true identity and who we pray and hope that upon reading this book may truly re-discover themselves and their identities. Man was created by God in His Own image:

man and woman created He them. Gen 1:27. That has never changed.

God is our Father but right from the Garden of Eden, we have been disobedient. Our First father Adam disobeyed the Law of God and so sinned against God and thus we acquired the sin nature from him. And like the DNA shows we are like our fathers. We as humans, black or white or yellow, inherited the sin nature from Adam. That sin nature pitted one of Adam's sons to kill the other. That same feature is playing out today all over the world as hatred resulting from jealousy, envy, greed, avarice, which pitted one child of Adam and Eve against the other, seeing the other not as a brother or sister but as an enemy to be exterminated.

Paul The Apostle, also a descendant of Adam and Eve like the rest of us, agonized over this contradiction in Romans 7: 19-20

(19 For the good that I would I do not: but the evil which I would not, that I do.

20 Now if I do that I would not, it is no more I that do it, but sin that dwelleth in me."

And here is the dilemma and the way out expressed in verses 24-25

(24 O wretched man that I am! who shall deliver me from the body of this death?

25 I thank God through Jesus Christ our Lord. So then with the

mind I myself serve the law of God; but with the flesh the law of sin."

And then offered the solution in Galatians 2:20

"I am crucified with Christ: nevertheless, I live; yet not I, but Christ liveth in me: and the life which I now live in the flesh I live by the faith of the Son of God, who loved me, and gave himself for me."

Therefore, the solution is not some psychology-based self-improvement project. The solution is *the exchanged life*, exchanging *the life of sin* with *the life of the spirit*. It is not a question of reformation but of salvation. It is the entering into *the resurrected life*. Only a resurrected life can live a holy life. The life that can resist sin and live in victory is the life, as Paul has shown, in which 'self' has died so that the new life is lived by *"the faith of the Son of God"*. It is a progressive death to self. Paul says: *"I die daily"*. (1 Corinthians 15:31). This is the life in which rebellion against God has ended and a new life lived in obedience to Jesus Christ has taken root.

The Identity Problem: Loss of Connection with the Creator

So how can there be an identity problem? Many people are just going through life without knowing who they are or where they are going. They live for the day. And because they are lost, they grope and stagger around in the dark, seeking to know who they truly are. This lostness is by choice. There is identity problem in a life that is in rebellion against God and has strayed away from Christ. The identity is recovered through repentance and submission to the Lord Jesus Christ. The prodigal misuse of his freedom must come to an end. The Prodigal must 'come to himself' and return home. Luke 15:1132. Even if you have never heard the Gospel, you see and hear God speaking every day in that every day *"the Heavens declare the Glory of God. Day unto day uttereth speech,"* (Psalm 19:1-6).

If a man walks in darkness, he will stagger. That is why the Word of God says: *"Your Word is a lamp unto my feet,"* (Psalm 119:105). *"Your Word have I hid in my heart that I might not sin against you,"* (Psalm 119:11). When you question the appropriateness or relevance of the Word of God for your life rather than believe the Word of God you are in rebellion. You have stepped from Light into darkness and you are bound to stagger like a drunkard. (Job 12:25).

The person who describes himself or herself as gay or a lesbian has a confused mind. The Mind is the battlefield. Unless you have the mind of Christ, Satan can take over your mind and make you lose your identity.

Here is a classic example of a confused mind describing how she came to 'rediscover' who she really was at the age of 36, in her own words. Here is a CNN report as follows

"By Melisa Raney, with illustrations by Ian Berry Updated 5:18 PM ET, Thu June 6, 2019

"By the time you reach your 30s, you think you know yourself -- your likes, your dislikes, what inspires you, what makes you tick. But there I was, at 36 years old, realizing I didn't know myself at all. I had everything I thought made my life perfect. I was married to my best friend and we had two beautiful, healthy and hilarious children, with successful careers and a beautiful home.

My life would change forever after a simple Google search in November 2016. I had just seen Kate McKinnon perform the song "Hallelujah" on SNL and discovered that she's a lesbian. That shocked me because she didn't fit the awful stereotype often depicted in the media.
I quickly declared her my "new girl crush." But it was more than that. At that moment, I realized that I wanted a relationship with a woman like her -- but I felt terrible for even having this thought, as someone who was faithfully married."

She watched a performance of a song and right away she fell in love with the singer and immediately wanted to be like her. Because the singer she likes is a lesbian she then decided to be a lesbian and immediately did away with her husband, her children and now has determined that if she would remarry in future it would be with another woman like herself!!!

How can you determine your true identity in front of a screen, hearing a song and liking the performance and the body of the singer? So, having those children was not her making. She was deceived by the real world. The make-belief television screen and the beautiful rendering of Alleluia song by a lesbian led her to know her true identity. She wanted to be like her. Her husband who was her best friend was not real. Her children were not really hers because she did not know herself then. For 36 years she slept and woke up to find that she had been pregnant twice and produced two Midwich cuckoos whom she did not own. Tomorrow she could become a transgender or any other hybrid and on and on like Quicksilver!

The basic sin is rebellion. It is in our sin nature that always questions God just as in the Garden of Eden. The devil observed that our Mother Eve did not really want to obey God and so tempted her by asking: Did God really say you should not eat of the fruit? Her answer showed that she already was poised to disobey. She told a lie. She answered the snake that God commanded them not even so much as to touch the fruit!

What about the Child who never had a chance to know God?

There are those who never had an opportunity of a father or mother to teach him or her the way of God, or who was never shown love? Indeed, there are possibly people who have never heard the Gospel of Jesus Christ even here in the US. So, as you are reading this you are asking how can they ever follow God's way. The way of God has been clear from Day 1 as well enunciated in Psalm 19. "The Heavens declare the Glory of God," (verse 1), is a universal message, quiet, unhidden and observable throughout the Universe. Everyone sees and hears that "Day unto Day uttereth Speech". (Verse 2).

During the first marriage, Jesus had not come. The Gospels had not been written or preached as we as we know it today but has been inherent in creation. God gave love through Creation and asked to be loved back through Obedience to the Creator. We chose to rebel. We had everything we needed but we were not satisfied by all that He gave but wanted to replace Him so we won't need Him.

There were those who chose to follow God in love and obedience among the children of God namely Abel, Seth and others. And there were those that disobeyed like Cain and his line. Of the descendants of Adam and Eve some were good, some were bad and so it is today and it is by choice.

There is no one who does not have the knowledge of God in Him but each has a choice to follow or to disobey. So, there are always those who would follow what is good and what is good is the way of Love. There is no challenge in relationship that Love cannot overcome. Love, genuine love is the basis of the success of Christian marriage. More of this later.

The Danger of Renaming Sin

Sin is a disease brought about by rebellion and, is curable by repentance and prayer of deliverance. God loves the gay, the lesbian, the pedophile, the promiscuous adulterer, the greedy and deceitful politician, the compulsive liar, as He loves every sinner and the Church on earth should love them as well.

All those sins have been cancelled by Jesus Christ Who paid the Price for the sins with His Blood shed on the Cross of Calvary. So, the path to recovery and cure is not through conversion therapy but through repentance, salvation and prayer of deliverance in the Name of Jesus.

The process begins with a change of vocabulary. Call a spade a spade not a 'gardening orientation instrument'. Adultery is "Adultery" not extra "marital sex". What was wrong with what God called it "Adultery"? Nothing. It is a clear term and the sin it calls adultery is clear. The same desire to satisfy self rather than obey God is behind questioning what God calls adultery. Did God really call it Adultery? YES. Does not that really mean sexual orientation. No. Sexual orientation does not mean anything definite. It means what you want it to mean. It is an all-inclusive term that can accommodate incest, pedophilia as the new norm. It is straight from the language of George Orwell's Science fiction titled 1984 in which the new meaning of War is Peace and vice versa.

Homosexuality is not sexual orientation. It is homosexuality. Period. If you start by not trying to launder evil words to become acceptable, that would be a good beginning because then, you will have to confront the issues these words convey rather than accept the anesthetic version that detonates the poisoned words without letting you feel the pain.

So now having stated the Kingdom principles upon which this book is based we shall proceed to discuss the Kingdom process of finding your spouse.

PART ONE

FINDING YOUR SPOUSE

Reader, please be reminded that this book is addressed to the person who knows his or her identity. However, if you are not sure of this, it is necessary to check it out. Let me illustrate this important factor by reference to the protocol for marriage in Royal families especially the British royal family.

Marriage in the British Royal Family

The heir to the throne cannot just independently determine who he or she is going to marry. Today an ordinary member of the public can meet someone on the bus and within a few days both can walk to the city hall and can just get married. Not so if you are a member of the British Royal family

No, the heir to the throne must first submit the proposal to the Royal Council for approval. What is the explanation for this procedure? Part of this is historical. In the olden days, Kings led their armies to war. We have read the stories of Kings leading their armies to battle from time immemorial. So, the king has to be physically strong. The royal line cannot afford to have pollution of the royal blood line. The royal council would check on the identity of the spouse. Are there any degenerative diseases running in the proposed spouse's family line? Is there any criminal record that can taint the Crown if he or she is brought into the royal line?

Not only that, the royal family has to be a model to the rest of the nation in every way possible, in moral standing and integrity. So, the Royal Council would want to make sure there is no known slander, shameful and disgraceful act pertaining to the genealogy of this proposed spouse. Like Caesar's wife, he or she must be above board.

In relatively recent history of the Monarchy in Great Britain, there was an heir to the throne who became king as a bachelor. Upon becoming King, he disclosed that he had fallen in love with an American divorcee. Here is the story:

Born on June 23, 1894, Edward VIII was a popular member of the royal family and heir to the throne. In 1931, then known as the Prince of Wales, Edward met and fell in love with American socialite Wallis Simpson. After George V's death, the prince became King Edward VIII. However, because his marriage to Simpson, an American divorcée, was forbidden, Edward abdicated the throne after ruling for less than a year. Thereafter, he took the title Duke of Windsor and embarked on a jet-setting life with his new wife. He died in France in 1972.

Incidentally the King or Queen of England is legally the head of the Church of England and the Church does not permit divorce. For these reasons an heir is not free to treat seeking a spouse and getting married as a casual matter. It is of paramount importance to the monarchy because the prince or princess who is heir to the throne does have a special identity that dictates how he or she would go about connecting with a spouse and must follow the laid-down process to obtain an approval. Getting a spouse and getting married have implications for matters beyond his or her own immediate personal interest or pleasure.

Marriage in My Culture—Back in the Day

Even in many non-western communities of the world, this age-old practice still exists outside royal families. After I got married to my wife I found out that when my then wife to be had gone to inform her father that she wanted him to meet the person who had proposed marriage to her, her father had asked for my name, city in which I was born and the names of my parents. He then asked her to give him some time and would indicate to her a suitable date to meet with me.

It was after we got married that my wife shared with me the steps her father later disclosed to her, he had taken before giving his approval. I learnt that he had ordered an investigation through trusted family emissaries to find out such matters as to whether any major disease might have been associated with my family line in the community; how male members of my family line were known to treat their wives and if there were any disgraceful and antisocial activities associated with my family line. It was upon obtaining a clearance on those issues that my father-in-law gave approval to meet with me!

In other family matchmaking traditions in some other non-western communities and countries, the above factors were usually the major considerations for families to come together to determine spouses for their wards. Arranged marriage is most prominent in India and South Asia and this form of marriage has been found to be most stable especially among the Amish, orthodox Jews and Hindus for instance.

You may ask how this is important in today's world where technology is there to reveal all about anyone. After all, one is living today in a world of individual freedom. And one has opportunities to check things out before tying the knot such as Christian websites, Christian blind dates, medical reports etc.

Marriage in the Royal Family of the King of kings and Lord of Lords

This is where the issue of identity comes in. The Bible describes the *believer* as living in this world but that he or she is actually not of this world. Believers belong to the Kingdom of the Lord Jesus Christ, the Kingdom that superintends over all the kingdoms on the earth. In that Kingdom, there is never a mis-match in marriage if the *believer* follows the protocol of the Royal Priesthood. We cannot follow the methods of the world system in which we are ambassadors of the Kingdom of God. Reader, the beautiful thing about this Kingdom is that if you are not yet a member, you can become one even now.

All you need to become a member of the Royal Priesthood is to acknowledge the truth that you, like "all" of the people of the world, have sinned and come short of the glory of God and also to know that your sins, as well as those of the world, have been forgiven!. You need to admit that truth, repent of your sins and receive the freedom already paid for on the Cross of Calvary where the precious blood of Jesus was spilled as payment for your sins and the sins of the world. Now whoever is willing, can receive the free gift of salvation, and follow Christ in order to live a life of freedom from the power of sin. Whoever accepts Jesus Christ as His personal Lord and Savior, is saved from the power of sin and has become the son or daughter of God.

I am not inviting you here to a life improvement project that will make you by self-will to follow a process of making you a better person. No. I am inviting you to an exchanged life. You exchange your life with the life of Christ. The process is not easy but it is simple. Once you believe the Truth that you are a sinner, it is easy to know that the Law of the Creator of the Universe is that the soul that sins must die. Jesus has paid for the sins that you have committed and will commit. The only way you can exercise authority over sin is to let the Holy Spirit live in you and exercise that authority, because the Holy Spirit is the Spirit of Christ in you. And He will come into you upon surrendering your life to Jesus. That step changes your status and your identity

Your old self dies and you put on Christ such that the life you now live is that of Jesus Christ living inside of you. It is not possible for you or anyone to live a life of obedience or holiness to God by will power. You cannot live a life of Holiness by will power or through a self-improvement project.

It is through voluntary submission. Once you believe the Truth that you are a sinner, it is easy to know that the Law of the Creator of the Universe is that the soul that sins must die. Now Jesus has paid for the sins that you have committed and will commit. Now the only way you can exercise authority over sin is to let the Holy Spirit live in you and exercise that authority, because the Holy Spirit is the Spirit of Christ in you. And He will come into you upon surrendering your life to Jesus. That step changes your status and your identity. You are now a child of God!

With this new status, you are no longer your own master, no longer your own god and have now been freed from the power of sin. You now belong to Master Jesus; you are "born again" and now a new Royal member of His Kingdom, the Kingdom that would never end. You are no longer under the satanic power of the flesh where satan was always pushing you to lust after the wrong things that destroy both the soul and the body. You are now truly freed by the power of the Holy Spirit, the Spirit of God that is now resident in you. So, what does that mean? It means you have a new identity verified by the Holy Spirit the unassailable and perfect 'Chip' in you Who has become your GPS *'God's Positioning System'* from now on.

If you desire to marry, you just need to follow the Kingdom process. Your feeling and your desire to get married are in response to God's Mind when He created you and me. In the Book of Gen. 1: 26-

27, God had created Man on day 6. Every creature that God created earlier, God brought to Adam for him to name each of them. Whatever Adam called the name of the creature it is the name it has borne since. But then God said none of those creatures was fit to be Adam's companion. And yet God had declared that it was not good for man to be alone. Although Adam was surrounded by all types of creatures and mammals in the forests, God saw that Adam was still 'alone' because none of those creatures was fit to be Adam's companion.

We should follow the culture and dictates of the Kingdom to which we belong. The Lord Jesus Christ is the Head of the Kingdom to which we belong here on earth. The first guideline of the Kingdom for choosing a spouse is that marriage is between a man and a woman. For the child of God there is no confusion of identity. You are either a man or a woman. There is nothing that a man created as man and a woman created as a woman need to discover further. You cannot be a male, who was born as a male or a female born as a female to now go on a voyage of rediscovery to rediscover his or her true identity to know who he or she is truly is!

Departure from God's Established Order Results in a Slippery Slope

The ridiculous extent of the so-called 'self-discovery' is illustrated by the recent confession of a woman and a mother of two, one Melissa Raney who in a CNN report of June 6, 2019 reported that she suddenly discovered that she was gay. At age 36 and with two children born by her as a woman, a wife and as mother suddenly realized that she "didn't know myself at all".

She came to know herself after watching "Kate McKinnon perform the song "Hallelujah" on SNL and discovered that she's a lesbian." She suddenly realized "that I wanted a relationship with a woman like her". That was the amazing story of self-discovery at age 36. And that self-discovery had led to walking away from her husband and two children in order to be free to be herself. And she added that if she would marry again, she would marry a woman. For 36 years she did not know that she was a 'man' but had two children as a woman nonetheless, but is now ready to marry a woman. Is this phenomenon akin to psychogenic amnesia? Psychogenic amnesia is a disease. Gay like any other sin is a disease and all these diseases need healing and are curable by the Power of the Cross.

Some Pseudo-scientists have argued that homosexuality is not a disease and that the story of the centurion of Capernaum (Matthew 8.5-13) shows that. Here is a gay pastor commentator on that Text:

> "We have the situation of a Roman centurion, whose slave
> is paralyzed. It is obvious to some that the centurion has a
> very special relationship of love with his slave (or boy as
> he is called several times in the text). In any case, Jesus
> heals the slave from his paralysis, but not from his
> homosexuality."

Before this word was introduced here, there was no reference to "homosexuality" at all. She simply asserted here the term 'homosexuality' as if it is a self-evident fact. There was no premise indicator That is not only a dishonest sleight of hand in writing but it is patently a false statement.

The Bible did not use that word or that disease in the quoted story. However, if you assert that Jesus did not heal that disease, then you have admitted that the Bible categorizes homosexuality as a disease only that in this case Jesus did not heal the disease. So, it necessarily follows from the logic of this presentation not only that homosexuality is a disease and that it can be healed, only that Jesus did not heal the boy of the disease nor for that matter, the boy's father. "Jesus loves his disciples and was always with them." However, there is no logic here in this gay advocate writer. The slave was paralyzed. That was what was obviously brought to Jesus and he was healed of that ailment. There was nothing about homosexuality in that story and you cannot manufacture one to justify your position

There was another man who obviously so loved his son that he had taken him to several places to find cure for him. Was this father then having a homosexual or incestual relationship with his son by reason of his love and devotion to his son? Such an academic perversion is an indication of the depravity and lack of integrity in the discussion on this subject matter by the defenders of what is essentially an abomination. In this rendition the definition of *love is sex, including a non-natural and perverted sex.* The greatest love story is the story of the Cross not a story of sex.

However, this small guidebook is not about the subject of homosexuality nor of rare diseases and their cure. It is about people of the Kingdom of God who know their God and follow the guidance of the Holy Spirit to find a spouse. In the scenario of the British monarchy stated earlier, the royal Council for the believer, is constituted by God the Father, God the Son and God the Holy Spirit. This is the Holy Trinity. The Executive Officer is the Holy Spirit. You will find the Royal Council in the book of Beginnings: Genesis Chapter 1: 1-3, quote scripture fully namely God, His Spirit, the Holy Spirit and the Word – Jesus Christ.

To have God as Your "Father-inLaw", Marry one of His Children

Here are the Operating instructions of the Royal Council, that is The Holy Trinity on finding a spouse. In the spouse search, it is the man who *finds* while the woman prepares herself to be *found*. Listen to this:

"He who finds a wife, finds a good thing and obtains favor of the Lord." (Proverbs 18:22). He must first find in order to receive the favor. Should a woman make the proposal? According to God's model of

marriage, the answer is No. The man or the family of the man makes the approach. That is the pattern laid down by God and followed throughout the Bible by people of The Covenant.

Abraham followed this process to find a wife for Isaac his son. See Genesis 24:1-33.

"1 And Abraham was old, and well stricken in age: and the Lord had blessed Abraham in all things.

2 And Abraham said unto his eldest servant of his house, that ruled over all that he had, Put, I pray thee, thy hand under my thigh:

3 And I will make thee swear by the Lord, the God of heaven, and the God of the earth, that thou shalt not take a wife unto my son of the daughters of the Canaanites, among whom I dwell:

4 But thou shalt go unto my country, and to my kindred, and take a wife unto my son Isaac.

5 And the servant said unto him, Peradventure the woman will not be willing to follow me unto this land: must I needs bring thy son again unto the land from whence thou camest?

6 And Abraham said unto him, beware thou that thou bring not my son thither again.

7 The Lord God of heaven, which took me from my father's house, and from the land of my kindred, and which spake unto me, and that sware unto me, saying, Unto thy seed will I give this land; he shall send his angel before thee, and thou shalt take a wife unto my son from thence.

That instruction is repeated in new form in 2 Corinthians 6:14 King James Version (KJV)

14 Be ye not unequally yoked together with unbelievers: for what fellowship hath righteousness with unrighteousness? and what communion hath light with darkness.

The import of this instruction is that a believer in Christ must seek to find his or her spouse within the Christian Community of Faith. During pre-marital counseling, one issue frequently raised, is this that if one knows this friend is a good guy or a good lady and I believe that he or she would eventually become a Christian because I believe that he or she actually loves me can we not commit to marry each other knowing that we are in love? And if we are not sure can we not live together to check things out for some time to see if it will work. This, I find, goes on even among church goers, a habit that is called 'shacking up."

To address this issue, I will like to refer to a line from Shakespeare's Macbeth, which states: "There's No Art to Find the Mind's Construction in The Face" The line is spoken by King Duncan in Act 1 scene 4 of Shakespeare's Macbeth. What this statement means is "that one cannot read someone else's mind by merely looking at his or her face. In short it means there is no way to predict betrayal". If there was such an art, every parent will rush for it especially for their daughters.

These days we have heard of cases of one spouse taking a heavy insurance cover for the other only to have him or her killed in order to claim the insurance money. There are many stories of men behaving as very good gentlemen only to show their true character after marriage. You can never be sure of the true nature of anyone by your own common sense. Now God who created men and women said of them in Jeremiah 17:9 "The heart is deceitful above all things, and desperately wicked: who can know it?" Since the heart of the King is in God's Hands Proverbs 21:1, it is much better to let Him reveal your spouse to you.

How I Found or Met The "Bone from My Bones"

Which then is the process to be followed by the man? First, the man goes looking in the right places. The right place is within the family of God, the Christian community of Faith. As we mingle, and someone catches our attention, we must quickly submit our emotions to The Lord to seek His guidance. Lord, is this the one?

I met my wife 48 years ago and I did just that. I had met with others before her. Sometimes I had rushed ahead before asking the Lord and had sometimes burnt my fingers only now to rush back to the Lord. Also, my parents were always praying for us their children concerning that and other things. Their constant prayer was that our lives would bring glory to the Name of The Lord. God heard that prayer. Three out of five of us became ordained ministers of the Gospel at different times on three continents!

When I found my wife, the Lord let me know that she was the one. We can hear the Lord through many different ways He chooses to speak to us. In order to hear Him we need to be familiar with His Voice. Jesus says in John 10:27; *"My sheep hear my voice, and I know them, and they follow me: …"* Jesus is the true Shepherd and we are *"the sheep of His Pasture"* (Psalm 100:3). We become familiar with The Voice of the True Shepherd, Jesus Christ as we spend time with Him in His Word and in Prayer. In Joshua 8: 8, God instructs us that *"This Book of the Lord must not depart from…..and that we must meditate upon it day and night so that we may prosper."* That is the path to all-round prosperity, not only financially but matrimonially, physically and emotionally.

To hear Him requires diligence that comes from the belief that without hearing Him, we are lost. God is a rewarder of them that diligently seek Him. (Hebrews 11:6). As we fellowship with the Master, and worship Him regularly and diligently, we become sensitive to His Spirit.

For instance, the Lord speaks to me mostly through dreams.

Sometimes however, the Lord impresses a notion on my heart as I read His Word or as I listen to a message. Sometimes He confirms a message through a prayer partner or our parents praying for us.

Sometimes our parents or loved ones may make a suggestion as to whom we might want to consider for a life partner. But whoever makes a loving suggestion or shares a revelation concerning this or any other matter, it is absolutely important that you seek confirmation from the Lord through His Word. The Lord will never contradict His Word. Therefore, any advice or revelation must be consistent with His Word. Listen to Him:

"Command me by my Word" (Isaiah 45:11). He keeps His promises, hence Psalm 138:2 *"you have exalted your Word above your Name."* Therefore, always the Word is it!

In my own case, my younger sister, concerned that I was still single at a time it seemed to all, I should be married, told me one day that she would want me to meet one of her close friends and that I would surely like her. So, a casual meeting was arranged "accidentally on purpose". Upon meeting her I immediately felt attracted to her. This was unusual because at that time and after being best man seven times, I had from various observations, come to the conclusion that marriage was perhaps not for me.

Of course, my friend's lots were exceptionally different, but I feared what if I fell into the other category. One of the reasons I had determined that marriage was not for me was the stories of infidelity I had been hearing from friends older than me. A small book by Bakare Gbadamosi and Ulli Beier had some effect on my imagination and my view of women at the time. It is a short Yoruba story titled *"Not even God is ripe Enough to catch a woman in love"*. In that story, a woman devised ingenuous ways to cheat on her husband without being caught even when the suspecting husband tried many ways to keep watch. Then finally I had a crush on a pretty girl of my age and simply adored her only to find she was very unfaithful and having affair with an older man. That did it!

I have always loved children but I was not going to get married just because of that. So, I decided that I would adopt children rather than marry. I had gone to the Motherless baby's home in Lagos Nigeria to adopt a baby. But there was one condition that I could not meet. It was that I must have a mother figure at home for the child who must be a live-in woman caregiver. First, I could not afford one at that time. Secondly that was to me at the time like getting married 'under false pretenses' so to say.

Therefore, it was quite surprising that I had this warm feeling towards my sister's friend. I must say however, that by this time, I had grown closer to God through, I believe, my parents' prayers and my growing love for the Word and a more consistent prayer life. So, I went to my father to disclose this interest and requested him to please seek the Face of The Lord along with me. Of course, two of my closest friends knew about this, met her and felt drawn to her and have been very close to her ever since. However, I needed a confirmation that this thing was not just my flesh and that it was pleasing to God. Here is how I prayed to God and have prayed for my children about their spouses ever since:

> "Lord please if this is not your wish, cancel it even if
> everyone around me says this is the best choice for me.
> Also, Lord if this is your wish, even if everyone around me
> says this is not right, Lord let your will be done. I do not
> want to go on this journey on my own. I do not want this if
> you are not in it, Lord, please."

Then my father sent for me and told me that he had been praying to the Lord concerning my request and that in his dream in answer to my prayer he found himself singing the following Hymn: "There shall be showers of blessings, this is the Promise of love."

See the following Scriptures as you pray the blessings down: Psalm 115:12; Ezekiel 34:26; Genesis 32:26:

There shall be showers of blessing:
This is the promise of love;
There shall be seasons refreshing, Sent
from the Savior above.

Refrain:

Showers of blessing,
Showers of blessing we need: Mercy-
drops round us are falling, But for
the showers we plead.

There shall be showers of blessing,
Precious reviving again; Over
the hills and the valleys,
Sound of abundance of rain.

Refrain:

There shall be showers of blessing;
Send them upon us, O Lord;
Grant to us now a refreshing, Come,
and now honor Thy Word.

Refrain:

There shall be showers of blessing:
Oh, that today they might fall, Now
as to God we're confessing, Now
as on Jesus we call!

Refrain:
There shall be showers of blessing,

If we but trust and obey; There
shall be seasons refreshing, If we
let God have His way.

Refrain:

Confirmed, I went straight to my girlfriend and declared that The
Lord had spoken. We are meant for each other. I proposed marriage
and I thought she would rush at this thing but she answered me calmly
that, that was good but that she needed to hear as well from the Lord.
And she kept me waiting for good nine months! It was tantalizing and
puzzling to me at the time, but waited I did.

Finally, she said, "Yes, I Will Marry You"

Then that day came. She had got the confirmation. Yes, she gladly
accepted the engagement ring. She was pleased but then she made a
curious request that we should go back to the jeweler from whom I
purchased the engagement ring. I was wondering why. Was the ring
not good enough? We got to the Jeweler. And she took a look at others.
I noticed she was looking from among the cheaper ones to choose
from. I could not believe she would do that.

When we left the jeweler with the new engagement ring on her
finger. She stopped and looked at me straight in the face and the ring
and made the following unforgettable statement: 'Bisi', her favorite
name for me, "this ring is not what will make our marriage work. It is
just a symbol of something much greater - Love in Christ," or words
to that effect.

I can never forget that moment. So as far as she was concerned,
external trappings, money or lack of it, fame or lack of it, would not
have any effect on what the Lord had put together. The story of our
relationship has continuously affirmed that position. We had gone
through many ups and downs and several times we had hurt each

other, without the children ever noticing anything. It was the Truth that God was in the relationship from the beginning and affirmation moments such as the above and others referred to in this short book that kept us focused on the Rock of ages.

God speaks to us in dreams and more often to my wife audibly. So, one day she shared with me the revelation that the Lord showed concerning our relationship as a result of which she accepted my proposal. After she had prayed for direction on the matter, one day The Lord showed her how the journey of our relationship would be.

In her dream we were to cross a big gorge on a very narrow bridge that would not take more than 2 people walking side by side. Many wild animals were deep below and howling threateningly. We could not see them but we had better not look down; we would fall! As we were walking towards this narrow bridge, the noise of the animals became more threatening and frightening. There was a man at the beginning of the bridge, in a white garment, holding a shepherd's staff. As the howling of the threatening animals continued, this shepherd stretched the staff in his hand to the animals. Suddenly they kept quiet and suddenly we arrived at the other end of the long bridge. The scenery at the other end was so peaceful and beautiful with the sun radiating through the luscious vegetation.

So, that was why and when she came to me with a YES! No doubt my wife believed when I told her I had a confirmation from the Lord, but it was interesting that that she insisted that she also had to hear from The Lord before she would answer Yes or No.

Today I can testify that the journey these forty-seven years had been playing out that way. Many times, along this journey, either just getting out of one challenge or just going into one, we had heard the howling wolves and lions, but we also had remembered the Shepherd and His staff. Each episode after the other, we had had to remember that we did not embark on this journey on our own.

We had chosen to trust God for each other and to focus not on the howling ferocious animals but on the Rock of Ages represented by that elderly man in the dream, who with his shepherd's staff silenced the prowling wild animals, waiting for us to fall into their mouths below. Keeping our eyes on the Shepherd kept us from falling. He will also keep you from falling if you determine to follow God's narrow road by seeking your spouse through following the narrow road of obedience.

The point of this testimony is this that if you go into any relationship without submitting the process to the guidance of the Holy Spirit, then you are on your own. And frankly you do not want to be on your own in a relationship that is meant to be irrevocable. If you entered into the program as a result of computer matching, some other human matchmaking, unknown factors may dislodge the relationship.

Finding or Meeting Your Future Life Partner

I am not condemning visiting online dating sites, but I am saying that whatever search parameter is used cannot control for possible mismatch problems that may arise later. You must first of all submit your date to the guidance of the Holy Spirit.

Yes, there will be problems. There will be howling wild animals along your way. It is not a question of *if* there is, it is a question of *when*. When that time comes you do not want to be on your own. You want to be able to pray with confidence and claim that "Lord you were in this from the beginning, help us." You will be able to pray a prayer of agreement, rather than try to pray against each other. Do not be like the celebrities who in an attempt to control for unknown factors carry out pre-nuptial contracts.

Marriage is not a business contract. It is a covenant. Marriage is until death do us part. This testimony has shown the path to an enduring relationship in which God is our Father who brought us together.

Let God our Father be your Matchmaker.

Now, how should the lady prepare?

You will find in Genesis 24, how a wife was found for Isaac, the child of promise. It is extremely important to dwell on this story for the following reasons.

- It shows where Rebecca, who became Isaac's wife was found and how she was found.

- It shows that like Isaac, you, as a believer, are a child of Promise.

- It illustrates where a young lady who desires marriage should be found and in which state of being, she is to be found.

- It shows that the woman is found and not the other way around as it happens often today.

- It correlates with the Creation story. Adam was first created, then Eve from Adam's side and God brought Eve to Adam. The story of Rebecca's finding illustrates how a woman should be ready preparing to be a wife and a mother-in-waiting.

For every Eve, there is an Adam. For every woman who desires to marry, there is an Adam that God had created for her. But how does she get found by that Adam?

First, ladies must not feel ashamed to admit that they wish to get married. I have spoken to quite a number in Church over the years, who have adopted the approach that they really do not care much about marriage, whereas they really do. These are ones that are quite successful in their jobs and even occupy responsible positions in one ministry or the other in their Local Assemblies.

Their attitude is that they are already successful without a man so, it cannot be that necessary for them. They suffer privately but are quite stoical about it. Perhaps, as an escape, there have arisen in Churches the Singles Ministry for women, headed by women.

I am not aware of God's calling for anyone to be a single woman or

a single man or God saying 'Behold disciple, you are called to Singleness.' There is no need for any woman to be ashamed to admit that she wishes to get married. If a woman is privately praying for a husband, there is no need to feel ashamed of admitting her need of a husband. Your desire to get married is in keeping with the perfect will of God. He created man and woman, blessed them and said to them: *"be fruitful and multiply and replenish the earth."* (Genesis 1:28).

But is it mandatory for a woman to get married? Not really. If your desire is solely to be free to serve the Lord, then yes you can choose to be single for that purpose only. 1 Corinthians 7:25-40. However, the desire to remain single has to be genuinely because you are committed to giving God all your time; not because since you have waited for so long, you are giving marriage up out of frustration. Matthew 19: 8-12. In effect, when you are single, you have freedom to pursue the service of God with devotion and holiness while waiting rather than pining for when a spouse will come.

So, what does the single woman who desires to get married do to advance that course? If you desire to get married, then you need to learn to wait. Rebecca, Isaac's wife was found while she remained in her family home, carrying out her responsibilities faithfully as a daughter and sister. Therefore, you do not need to hurry out of the family home because you want to be free to make it easier to go on dates. God knows where you are. He knows your address and as you wait where you are, He will direct the man to you whom He has created for you just as He brought Eve to Adam in Genesis 2:22. Our main mission as a disciple is to grow daily in intimacy with Him so as to become more and more like Him.

A woman waiting to be found for marriage must keep herself pure as she waits. Her purity is a gift to be nurtured and should be protected. Rebecca was at home where she was found. The woman who wishes to marry should remain in the family, and or remain within her community of faith keeping herself in purity and seeking intimacy with the Lord. The husband for the waiting bride is located inside Christ. It is in seeking intimacy with the Lord that the woman will be found by the husband God has created for her.

A waiting bride is not to wait in idleness pining for a lover. She should wait trusting the Lord and pursuing what The Lord wants her to do. The Lord has a purpose for each individual. It is our duty to seek to know that purpose and to pursue it because our desire as followers of Jesus Christ is to seek to please Him in all our ways. Everything we are or do is of the utmost interest to our loving Father in heaven. The Bible says whether we are eating or drinking we should do so as unto the Lord. (1 Corinthians 10:31).

There was a senior colleague of mine whose daughter was in the nursing school who once expressed to me that her desire from her youth was to be a lawyer. First, she did not meet the entry requirement in English Language for admission into the School of Law. So, with her father's urging she settled for nursing so that she could finish in time and get married. In the meantime, she had become a born again Christian but her father was not yet born again at the time. When I came to know about it, I counseled her and her daddy as follows:

> If the Lord has placed a burden on your heart, you would
> not be at ease until you fulfill it. This is how you would
> know if a burden is the Lord's burden or your own self-
> imposed burden. When the burden is not lifted no matter
> how you want to dismiss it, it is most likely a burden placed
> on your heart by the Lord. You have tried to push this law
> study away because of some huddle in the way and so you

elected a shorter program so you would quickly be ready for a husband. The path to an all-round prosperity is obedience.

When you gave your life to the Lord Jesus Christ, you had immediately become enlisted into the Army of God and signed away the right to yourself, you are now owned by Another, Jesus Christ, who is now the Director of your life. I also advised her that she was now married to Jesus and that her husband is located inside Christ in and through Whom there would be a divine connection.

To the glory of God, she followed the counsel, recommitted her life to the Lord Jesus Christ, went back to school, met her English language requirement, and got admission to the Law School. It was in the process of that change of direction where she was divinely connected with a man who later became her husband. And the Lord had blessed her in her law profession as a Professor of Law and for some years now have been helping a West African Country (The Gambia) serving, on contract as a judge of the Court of Appeal even as of January 2017 to help them to establish a righteous Judicial system in that country, to the Glory of God.

It was in the path of obedience that she found her husband and also found fulfillment in the ministry that The Lord had prepared for her from the foundation of The World. When you follow the Kingdom principles, you become an overcomer as a member of the Royal Priesthood, a child of the Most High God.

What about Dating?

Now that you are developing a relationship with someone and waiting to see if you are meant for each other, how do we relate during this waiting period in a way that shows that we are children of the Most High God, and members of the Royal Priesthood?

Again, realizing and reminding ourselves of our identity is the key to how we date. That means that you cannot date somebody outside the family of God, that is, the born-again Christians. Of course, you can be a friend to someone who may not be a believer but you cannot date such a person. We are to love everyone and we are to bring the Good News of the Kingdom to all in our sphere of influence but we cannot have a dating relationship with anyone unless both of you are committed to the Lord Jesus Christ and committed to growing in Him.

What about someone in your church? Because someone attends church does not mean that that person is committed to Christ. As you wait for someone God may be bringing your way, the waiting bride needs to watch and pray. A committed Christian will seek to see if the person she is being drawn to is committed to growing in his relationship with God. Whoever is not growing is dying.

How do you know somebody is growing? First is character. By their fruits we shall know them. It does not matter if the person is a Pastor or a Pastor's son. What is he "preaching" with his life? Actually, every Christian is a preacher whether at work or in church. Everywhere we are at work or at a play is a pulpit and we are preaching. What are we preaching and what are we observing being preached to us? Are we seeing a reflection of Christ? We can hardly have an answer to that question unless we ourselves are in Christ. The Holy Spirit will always lead us to the Truth. Jesus has assured us that the Holy Spirit *"will guide you into all Truth"*. (John 16:13)

What if you have a friend in church, in a fellowship, or ministry service activity or through a community or social interest group or some other platform and you get to like him or her. Great. What do you do about that? First examine yourself. Is this physical attraction?

Is it lust for that? Or this person may be attracted to you and you do not really find him attractive.

Remember you no longer belong to yourself. The question you take to the Lord is: Father, this person appears to like me; is this the one you have chosen for me? And as you pray, you watch to see if this person loves Jesus and if he is growing in his love for Christ. The watching is to see if the character bears fruit and the prayer seeks the approval of The Lord.

One of the things to watch is whether he is interested in marriage or just wants to play. The truth is, it is a good desire to want to get married and that should be the only focus of dating. However, the bride in waiting must be pure and faithful to God; the bed must be kept green as in Song of Solomon 1:1. One practical way to ensure that is that you are not left alone in an enclosed place. Be visible outside. Not only must you be holy but you must be seen to be holy.

There was one case where a father was very livid with her daughter when he learnt that her daughter passed a night in her boyfriend's apartment. The daughter was equally very sad that her father appeared not to trust her when she said nothing untoward happened and that the young man was a good Christian.

I reminded her of the common saying that 'Justice must not only be done but must be seen to be done'. The Bible says, *"let not then your good be evil spoken of"* (Romans 14:16). That is what that means. I know this young lady was very fervent for the Lord, so I said to her:

> "I know you go on evangelism and you counsel those who
> have just come to the faith. Supposing in the morning as
> you came out of your boy friend's apartment, you were met
> with a young believer you had just preached holiness to?
> What thought do you think will cross her mind? He or she
> might begin to wonder: "Is this thing really true". No, you

must run away from every appearance of evil." (1 Thessalonians 5:22).

Incidentally, she listened and slowed down seeking God's Face in the relationship. Eventually it did not last and the right person came along much later and they are, as I speak, happily married and are continuing to grow steadily together in the Lord.

One mistake children of God make in dating is that young Christian women are looking forward to being dated by someone as or more educated than they or who are from prominent families or someone who is highly educated. No, we should not focus primarily on those features. The question when we are approached or when we are attracted to someone is immediately to turn our emotions and feeling quickly to the Lord and ask: "Lord, is this the one?" That is the way never to make a mistake.

One of my daughters came up with a problem once. She had three suitors simultaneously and did not know what to do. One appeared to be head over heels in love and tried to let her know she was quite financially comfortable as a professional in his young age. We said to her we did not know whom she should choose or even if she should choose any of them. We advised her to fast and pray and ask our Father in heaven. She did. And soon the three quietly moved away from her life. The Lord is a rewarder of them that diligently seek Him.

Premarital Counseling—Equipping Yourself for "Two Becoming One"

Now when it appears that you have been "found", and you know that this man is the choice of the Lord for you, both you and the intending husband must attend Biblical counseling called *pre-marital counseling*. Is Pre-marital counseling really necessary? Yes. When you are now sure that you are meant for each other, one gets excited about the new relationship. However, this is the point that it becomes vitally important that you are instructed or get reminded about God's view of marriage, the Biblical Truth about Marriage. This is the time to know the difference between marriage according to the standard of the world and marriage according the Standard of The Kingdom to which we belong. There is need to explain to the newly engaged, the Biblical Principles that govern the roles of the wife and the husband as they relate to each other, their prospective children and their in-laws.

The new couple to-be need guidance about family finance, household responsibilities, bringing up of the children according to Kingdom principles. They have not been at this point before and need guidance how to traverse the new terrain. One's friend's pattern or even one's parents' pattern of marriage cannot be good enough guide. God Himself established marriage. Marriage was not formulated by man. Man did not design it. It did not evolve as a cultural evolution from Society. So, we cannot get the guidance from a book of Psychology or Sociology. The guidebook is the Holy Bible.

There is no doubt that challenges will arise along the journey. First you know that each of your heard from God and so you did not go into the relationship relying solely on your common sense or computer matching. So, God is with you. But then you need Biblical guidance on how to face challenges together and trust the Lord together. When issues arise and opinions clash, how do you deal with such situations when they arise?

Love and marriage constitute a wonderful mystery. Imagine: two different people from two different families, two different backgrounds, perhaps two races and even two different continents come together, fall in love and covenant to live together in a relationship as husband and wife "until death do us part". What can make this work is not similarity of professions, similar socio-economic backgrounds, comparable educational qualifications, secure financial resources or computer program matching. Similarly, both may come from the same country, the same city or town and even be cousins; it does not guarantee that the relationship will endure. The basic requirement for a lasting union is that the union is founded in Christ, remains in Christ and is sustained by Christ.

You may say, *"Preacher all these sounds well and good, but I am sure I am a child of God. My sins have been forgiven. I pray. I keep myself respectable and stay out of fornication but then I am in and out of relationships because the men even in church are hard to hold. You think things are going well but then they become suddenly unavailable."* One told me in tears: *"I was on with this guy and I thought I heard God but was shocked when the guy told me unless we have sex, he would not be sure that our relationship would work. I was devastated. I thought we were on the same platform in the same church!"* Yes, there are cases of the children of God who get "ghosted" and "bread crumbled" to use the phraseology of one Dr. Marni Feureman.

In a large church where once I was serving, the Lord opened my eyes to see that there were many young women who appear to love the Lord and who wished to get married. There were also many young men in that same Church who were apparently in a ready position to get married. But there was no connection. Then a Singles Ministry started, attended mainly by young women. The men did not attend that much. There were curriculum-based discipleship programs running for months at the end of which participants would receive certificates. The young people were comfortable with where they were. The trouble is that there was really no discipling going on. The elders appeared to prefer to "lecture" discipleship and get participants "qualified" as disciples and then feel ready to be "ordained" to ministries.

Discipling as Jesus did it and also as Rabbis did it before Christ came, takes the form stated in Mark 3: 13-14. That Jesus called the disciples that "they might be with Him" observing Him as He preached as He taught etc. It was not done by remote control nor through discipleship lectures online or simulation video courses. The

Kingdom way of discipling the young women in the Church is for the young women to observe the older women who are *"reverent in behavior, not slanderers or slaves to much wine. They are to teach what is good, and so* train the young women to love their husbands and children, *to be self-controlled, pure, working at home, kind, and submissive to their own husbands, that the word of God may not be reviled."* (Titus 3:2-5; 1 Timothy 5:2; emphasis, mine).

PART TWO

GETTING MARRIED

This chapter is not a counsel on how to set up for the wedding ceremony, or the wedding reception or where to go for your honeymoon or stuff like that. Remember, this union is made in Christ and sustained in Christ by the Power of The Holy Spirit. Therefore, Satan cannot be pleased. So, it will definitely try to bring challenges your way and we need to be on our guard and not give room for the enemy to creep in. In fact, we need to be on our guard to watch and pray together all through from the beginning of this journey until the very end. For illustration let us take a look at the Ministry of our Lord as He embarked upon it.

John the Baptist announced the Bridegroom, 'The Lamb of God', 'The Savior of the World' to the world by the side of River Jordan. The Trinity was present at the inauguration approving the launching of this unprecedented Ministry of Salvation. As Jesus, the 'Word of God', was going out of the water, having just been baptized, The Heavens opened, the Spirit of God descended like a dove upon His Head. And God spoke directly from Heaven for all to hear: *"This is my beloved Son in whom I am well pleased,"* (Matthew 3: 13-17).

The Holy Trinity will also attend your wedding if you invite the Trinity there. And it will be a peaceful and joyful event if you invite

Jesus there. Remember Jesus was invited to a wedding ceremony at Cana in Saint John's Gospel, Chapter 2:1-11. Remember that the guests included Jesus, His disciples and the Mother of Jesus. Whether Jesus will be there would depend upon who is being invited to your wedding party.

Doing All for the Glory of God

Since you are disciples of Jesus Christ the party would be made of your community of Faith and the "Greeks", that is, some God fearers who have heard about Jesus from you or have seen the life of the Jesus you preach in your life and by their coming are saying, as in John 12: 20-23, *"Sir, we will see Jesus."* What Jesus has done in each of your lives have been noised around and they have seen that. So, you have not attracted to your wedding party boasters, proud blasphemers' drunkards loud incontinent folks and the like: (2 Timothy 3:1-6). And as Jesus is there, there would be joy, he will turn water into wine. If party crashers of this kind crash in, they will be overwhelmed by the Presence of God and your wedding may provide a harvest of souls.

However, we must remember that after that awesome presence of the Trinity in the announcement of the Ministry of Jesus Christ Satan went on the attack. So, believe me, as you embark upon this journey walking on the narrow way, determined to follow Jesus Christ as His disciples, be prepared to resist the wiles of Satan. Just as Satan tried to derail the ministry of our Lord Jesus Christ, he will also try to derail your ministry. Yes, Marriage is a Ministry, the ministry designed to replenish the earth by bringing Godly seeds to the earth that we may have peace on earth.

As you begin the journey, think about the Garden of Eden. God would come in the cool of the day to fellowship with Adam and Eve. Genesis 3:5. But one day as God came to fellowship with them, they were nowhere to be found. They had let off their guard and fell into the trap of Satan. How did they do that? They shifted their focus from the Creator on to themselves and swallowed the bait of Satan that they could actually become their own god. That is the sin of Pride.

The Lust of the Flesh, the Lust of the Eyes and the Pride of Life

Satan tried Jesus with three temptations. The same temptations await your union. These are **Hedonism**, the temptation to focus on your personal physical satisfaction. In this case Satan tempted Jesus to use His Power to *"turn this stone to bread"* (Matthew 4:3); **Egoism:** The temptation to use your power to promote your self-importance. Jesus was tempted to flaunt His Power and show His Might. **Materialism:** use your power to acquire material things Actually all of these three temptations are exhibitions of the basic sin of Pride. But how can these temptations be manifest in our wedding plans, and how can they be warded off? These temptations can become manifest in our wedding plans, once we yield to the temptation to focus on the self and glorify self.

Hedonism and the Wedding Dress: In choosing the wedding dress, modesty is it! God expects the Christian woman to dress in *"modest apparel with propriety and moderation,"* (1 Timothy 2:9-10). Today, many young women have fallen into the sin of egotism by succumbing to the temptation to flaunt their bodies in an exhibition of what they see as the beauty of the body on their wedding day. It is often disheartening to watch this flaunting of bodies in Christian marriages conducted in the church of Jesus Christ. Half of the breasts and a good portion of the back is bare. Such public exhibitions of the self are unbecoming of a Christian lady. The desire behind such dressing is to impress all onlookers that you are physically very beautiful and to impress them with your body. It is an advertisement to the world inviting them to come and see how attractive you are and to have them desire your body.

Such advertisement of the body is the province of those who wish to 'sell' their bodies and want to attract attention of 'buyers.' It does not honor God nor the husband for whom the body of the wife is reserved to be seen and admired by him in the closet.

Such exhibition of the 'self' follows the world of "celebrities" who even show their naked bodies to the world through videos. The Bible states in 1 Peter 3:2-5 that beauty does not come from outward adornment but the hidden man of "the heart", the *"ornament of a meek and quiet spirit which is in the sight of God of great price"*. A frivolous exhibition of the body is cheapening the body, and neither honors God nor the husband that you have sworn to honor and to obey. Why should the husband cherish and hold that which has been advertised and exhibited as wares in the world market? The public already owns it.

We Are in the World, But not of the World

The Bible says we should do everything as unto the Lord. How can the flaunting of the sculptured body and the wearing of expensive jewelry be anything done unto our Lord who is *"meek and lowly"*? (Colossians 3:17). A beautiful woman is one who fears the Lord and that is what makes her attractive. Dressing is a reflection of the heart. If a woman dresses sensually and likes to be described as "sexy", then there is evil desire in her heart. To be sexy is to be "sexually attractive", *seductive, tempting, tantalizing;* that is to be sexually arousing. Why should you on the day of your wedding sexually arouse onlookers and thus turn their hearts away from God?

I know that going by what society does today, it is going to be difficult for a Christian lady to dress decently. A Christian lady will need the gift of discernment to make the right decision always. If you have inner strength which only Christ in you can provide, you will dress with dignity. The guard is this: all decisions we make should start with reminding ourselves of our identity. We are Royal Priesthood, sons and daughters of the Most High God. So, we are princes and princesses in the Kingdom of God. It is mandated that our Righteousness must exceed the Righteousness of the Pharisees. (Matthew 5:19-20). Take a look via Google at the weddings of Royals, even today and see how the brides dress. The World's Royal Household protocol requires the bride to be a model of excellence and decency in dressing. The child of an earthly King is a prince or princess, that is, a small 'King or Queen' and so must act as kings and queens, princes and princesses. Accordingly, they must carry themselves as models of excellence and decency in the world. In this practice the Kings and Queens of this world are supposed to be imitating us in Christendom. But we in the church descend to the level of commoners, whereas the kings, princes and princesses in the world, tend to rise above the common level.

Now God calls us His children. Since we are the children of God and therefore are princes and princesses God calls us gods in Psalm 82:6 i.e. *"Ye are gods"*, because *"all of you are children of the Most High."* But we are more than that. Like our Lord Jesus Christ, we are also priests, 1 Peter 2:5. Hence our group name of Royal Priesthood. The world system made up of the then leaders of the Covenant accused Jesus of calling Himself the Son of God. They said they were going to stone Him for that in John 10:30-36 thus:

"30 I and my Father are one.

31 Then the Jews took up stones again to stone him.

32 Jesus answered them, "many good works have I shewed you from my Father; for which of those works do ye stone me?"

33 The Jews answered him, saying. "For a good work we stone thee not; but for blasphemy; and because that thou, being a man, makest thyself God."

34 Jesus answered them, "Is it not written in your law, I said, Ye are gods?

35 If he called them gods, unto whom the word of God came, and the scripture cannot be broken;

36 Say ye of him, whom the Father hath sanctified, and sent into the world, thou blasphemest; because I said, I am the Son of God?"
KJV

In the Light of this Scripture, it is disgraceful that the world's Royal brides dress more decently in their weddings than the brides of God who get married in the Church of Jesus Christ today. And yet we are said to be the Light of the World.

So, as the temptation comes for you to flaunt your flesh and your jewelry, use the Word of God to resist Satan: "You shall not (cannot) live by bread alone, but by every word that proceeds from the mouth of God." No, you cannot feed the lust of the flesh. You cannot live on the admiration of the world but by every Word of God.

Egoism and the wedding Party: the temptation to display your wealth. Resist the temptation to show how rich and powerful you are by showing off your wealth at the wedding. Read this advice from the Fool, a character in Shakespeare's King Lear Act 1 Scene 4

"Have more than you show,
Speak less than you know, Lend
less than you owe.
Ride more than you walk…"

Good advice. And the Bible says we should not boast or show off. Just let us meditate on the two Scriptures below:

Jeremiah 9:23-26

23 Thus saith the Lord, let not the wise man glory in his wisdom,

neither let the mighty man glory in his might, let not the rich man glory in his riches:

24 But let him that glorieth glory in this, that he understandeth and knoweth me, that I am the Lord which exercise lovingkindness, judgment, and righteousness, in the earth: for in these things I delight, saith the Lord.

25 Behold, the days come, saith the Lord, that I will punish all them which are circumcised with the uncircumcised;

Also Proverbs 27:2

2 Let another man praise thee, and not thine own mouth; a stranger, and not thine own lips.

So again, here let your wedding party be moderate and devoid of boasting so that the Lord may be present and turn the Water into wine as in John 2:1-11. Confront the satanic temptation to flaunt your wealth with the Word of God that Jesus used at His temptation by resisting Satan with Deuteronomy 6:16 *"Ye shall not tempt the Lord your God, as ye tempted him in Massah."*

The third temptation is that of **Materialism**. There is the temptation even at your wedding party to use that opportunity to amass material things, plan for a big house, and expensive furniture and the like. Here also the appropriate guiding Word of God can be found in the following Scriptures:1 Cor. 6:12; Philippians 4:5

"Less is More"—My Wife and I Decided to Embrace Simplicity

In case you the reader wonder how my own wedding went, let me state here that even though I was Best Man for seven weddings, when it came to our turn, we intentionally did not have a wedding Party at all. Indeed, we did not print any wedding invitation or printed wedding ceremony programs. For crowd, it would have been payback time so to say for all the major actors in the previous weddings to return the compliment. Although, I had been in Radio Broadcasting at the time and we could have been sure of a crowd and also of media coverage. We informed only close family friends and only by word of mouth.

We had probably about 25 to 30 close friends and family members in all for the Church service. The priest used the portion of the Church Service book that dealt will the wedding service for the ceremony. We went from the Church Service straight for our honeymoon.

However, I must let you know that a week earlier we had had a traditional wedding. In most of Africa weddings in Christian communities is a mixture of traditional and modern Christian wedding. African traditional wedding is essentially a wedding of two families rather than of two individuals. The man pays the dowry. Since Africa was made up literally of agrarian communities, the prescribed dowry is made up of some money and farm products. In modern times, the bridegroom brings token farm products to the ceremony. On the appointed day, the family of the groom, including the extended family members accompany the groom to the family of the bride bringing the traditional requirements which normally includes, for the Christian a copy of the Holy Bible.

At the end of the first part of the ceremony which takes a whole day, when the dowry has been formally received and consent granted for the bride by her parents, the parents of the bride take the hand of their daughter and hand her over to the parents of the groom, not to the groom. When the family of the groom have received the bride on behalf of the groom, the family of the groom welcome the bride with dancing and prayers into her new family. Thereafter the groom is called forth and the two are prayed for by both families. And the next thing is that the bride is taken to the family home of the groom where welcome festivity awaits her and the groom. It is usually late evening and so it is joyful and short. In summary marriage in Africa is the marriage of two families.

Accordingly, since the bride was actually not handed over to the groom, he cannot unilaterally decide to divorce his wife. It must be a family decision. Similarly, the wife cannot solely decide she is packing out of her matrimonial home and return to her parents. The parents will not welcome her back. Therefore, divorce is rare, since the family will first intervene to resolve issues of disagreement until it appears unresolvable. Divorce is seen as a family disgrace. It is important to note that we had completed that traditional wedding before the Church event. But even the traditional wedding is an affair of two families and so not the kind of large crowds associated with the marriages among the elites of the Church today.

How Isaac Got His Bride

Now let us review the marriage of the child of promise, Isaac, Abraham's son. It contains the following elements: Isaac's parent sought for a wife for him within the family of Abraham not among the Philistines. Accordingly, a man must seek his wife from his family of born-again Christians. Secondly, the consent of the family of Rebecca was sought. Then the family asks Rebecca if she would accept the hand of Isaac. She agreed and then consent was given. Gifts were given by the groom and the parents of the bride also gave gifts to their daughter. It is interesting that marriage in Africa follows this pattern.

But the whole story of Isaac and Rebecca is a story of how God is interested in all the details of our lives. Gen. 24. It is the story of a young woman who was determined to trust and follow God wherever He is directing her. The whole plan to find a wife was soaked in prayer by Abraham, Abraham's servant Eliezer, and the parents of Rebecca. If we follow this pattern, we cannot fail. This is why we have always to remember our identity in making decisions about our wedding and wedding arrangements.

Now the temptation to show off is underpinned by the sin of Pride. and all that is underlined by the sin of Pride. When you scratch the surface of any sin, you are going to find pride under it. It was the basis of the sin of rebellion of our first father Adam to want to be like God even though he was already created in God's image and likeness.

There will surely come a temptation to lust after pomp and pageantry in planning for your wedding. I was best man seven times and attended several other marriages as guests before I got married. There is always the temptation to have large weddings at great expense especially if the participants are very educated and have good professional jobs. These occasions are also when parents want to show off. Some of the items for show are the engagement and wedding rings as if the monetary value or the rarity of the jewelry somehow conveys the depth of the love of the bridegroom and the extent the man is ready to make sure the marriage lasts forever. Nothing can be further from the truth.

There are too many cases of collapsed marriages of wealthy celebrities to show that those things do not guarantee a lasting relationship. Indeed, too many of these celebrity marriages have ended in one killing the other. Indeed, celebrity marriages have failed at least in the US more often than in any other group. In short, loud shows of affection neither necessarily indicate deep love for each other nor guarantee a lasting relationship. On the contrary, the louder the show the less likely it is to last.

PART THREE
STAYING MARRIED

Keeping the Vow— "For Better for Worse... Till Death Do Us Part"

You have just taken a vow that you have promised to keep. First, you must remember that what you have entered into is a covenant, not a contract. What is the difference? A contract says you agree to do this for me and that I will do this other thing for you. Contract is simply an exchange of promises. If you build my bungalow for me as designed by my architect, I will pay you an agreed amount of money. If one breaches the condition the contract is frustrated and ends.

However, a covenant is a perpetual irrevocable pledge made on oath. It is a *vow* or an *oath*. Therefore, a covenant is not vitiated even when one party breaches the condition of the Covenant. Each helps the other to be able to carry out his or her own oath. A covenant is a commitment which God initiates such as the covenant between God and Israel. And as we know Israel strays away from time to time just as today, we stray away from God from time to time. However just as God did to Israel, always drawing them back to Him (Hosea 2:4) even so today, God is always waiting for us as for the Prodigal son in Luke

15: 11-32, because He is the covenant keeping God. It is a perpetual Covenant.

God instituted Marriage not man nor society. God said it is not good for man to be alone and so created the woman and brought the woman to Adam who immediately declared: This is the bone of my bone and flesh of my flesh in Genesis 2: 18-23. So indeed, God conducted the first Marriage. He Himself joined them together. It is not a cultural development. The first thing to know is that we are, in marriage, on an irrevocable journey together.

Again, the marriage vow you have just made is made to God. You have covenanted with God "to love and cherish your wife or to "love and to obey" your husband. Your spouse is the beneficiary of the Covenant. The covenant is between you and God; you have vowed to God to keep your spouse. Now the Bible says in Ecclesiastes 5:4 *"When you vow a vow to God, do not delay paying it, for he has no pleasure in fools. Pay what you vow"*. And God to whom you have made the vow says that He hates putting away (Malachi 2:16). Accordingly, the first fundamental truth, or if you like, basic assumption that must govern your relationship is that you are committed to it all the way. It is a covenant.

The behavior of your spouse does not release you from the vow. The vow holds "until death do you part." Therefore, the word "divorce" must be considered anathema. If the couple are born again children of God and came together following the protocol stated in the first chapter of this little book, then there is no room for divorce. But as it will become clearer as we proceed in this discussion, you are not in a prison either. That divorce is not an option, may appear to you rather hard. Yes, you are not alone. The disciples of old who were with Jesus Christ thought exactly like you, (Matthew 19: 9-10). They said: *"If this is the case between a man and his wife, it is better not to marry."* As you would see as we proceed, God's ways are simple but not easy. However, the burden is light if you are *"yoked together"* with Christ.

The truth is this that marriage is not just about the pleasures of the here and the now. It is really about The Kingdom of Heaven. Jesus came to teach us about the Kingdom of God/Heaven and how to get there. You need to carry your cross and follow Jesus in order to get to heaven. That Path does not allow you to dump your spouse because you are finding the relationship rather inconvenient. Matthew 16:24 says: *"If anyone would come after Me, he must deny himself and take up his cross and follow Me"*

No Longer Two but One Flesh

One other element of this covenant is that both of you are now One. You cannot separate one from one, because to do that, will involve slicing the one in half! This truth of the Word of God was first enunciated in Genesis 2:24: *"Therefore shall a man leave his father and his mother and shall cleave unto his wife: and they shall be one flesh."* This Truth was also later confirmed in Matthew 19:4-6 and Mark 10:6-8, and by the Apostle Paul in Ephesians 5:30-32.

That principle of oneness is the sustaining strength in Christian marriage. Since the one is in the other as one flesh, you are inseparable from the other. Then it necessarily follows that if you are indeed one, then there is nothing that one knows and the other does not know. You are committed to "being naked together", being transparently open to each other. (Genesis 2:25).

In the beginning the couple (Adam and Eve), were both naked and were not ashamed. *"The man and his wife were both naked and they were not ashamed."* This means each hid nothing from the other. You might ask how about if the other hides something? That would constitute a sin against God with Whom we have covenanted to be one with our spouse.

Salvation, like marriage, brings us into a covenant relationship with God. We need to grasp the Truth that salvation is not about a character development program. It is not an invitation to a life improvement project. No, it is an *exchanged life*. Listen to Paul in his letter to The Galatians 2:20, KJV: *"I am crucified with Christ: nevertheless I live; yet not I, but Christ liveth in me: and the life which I now live in the flesh I live by the faith of the Son of God, who loved me, and gave himself for me."*

Actually, the call to salvation is a call to come and die to self. Period. So, both have to die to self, that is, die to the flesh. You will experience challenges on this journey that will put this new relationship on trial. It is not a question of 'If'. Trials will surely come, but as long as you trust Christ and He is allowed to be the focus of your relationship, you will always be an overcomer.

Jesus has shown us how to die to flesh and how to resist the temptation to give in to the flesh. Let's recall again the temptations of our Lord and Savior Jesus Christ in the wilderness. At the end of the temptations during which our Lord used the Word of God to defeat Satan at every turn, the Bible states *"And when the devil had ended all the temptation, he departed from him for a season."*

The devil departed only for a season! So, as you have overcome the temptations while you were planning your wedding, please remember that it is also for a season. After the temptation on the desert, Jesus suffered many temptations as recorded in Hebrew 4:15. And we too will suffer many. Trials come with the Call. (John 16:33). As David O. Mckay put it,

> "Now, when do temptations come? Why, they come to us
> in our social gatherings, they come to us at our weddings,
> they come to us in our politics, they come to us in our
> business relations, on the farm, in the mercantile
> establishment, in our dealings in all the affairs of life, we
> find these insidious working, and it is when they manifest
> themselves to the consciousness of each individual that the
> defense of truth ought to exert itself."

(David O. McKay, Conference Report, Oct. 1911, p. 59.)

The temptations continued until the very end even as far as Gethsemane. If these things could happen to Jesus, be ready also to have your Gethsemane experience on this journey. In all of the temptations, Jesus was tired but drew strength to resist the temptations from Word of God and The Holy Spirit. Overcoming the temptations and staying married follows the same process demonstrated by our Lord Jesus Christ all the way to Calvary.

Therefore, we overcome at every point by looking into the Word of God. *"Whoso looketh into the perfect law of liberty, and continueth therein, he being not a forgetful hearer, but a doer of the work, this man shall be blessed in his deed."* Such a couple will be blessed in their marriage.

Remaining One in Marriage by trusting God for one another

God Who created marriage is the all-knowing God of the Universe. He created man and He says about the man he created In Jeremiah 17:9 that his *"heart is deceitful above all things and desperately wicked, who can know it?"* And did not the Word warn in Micah 7:5: *"Do not trust in a friend. Do not put your confidence in a companion; Guard the doors of your mouth from her who lies in your bosom."* Is that not your spouse? How can we be consistently one?

Remember you are one in Christ. You do not have to trust the other, but you must trust God for the other. You found your spouse inside Christ. Your relationship can only be sustained inside Christ. Just keep your pledge and then intercede for the other that he or she may stand. The more intimate you are with Christ the closer you would be with your spouse. Imagine an equilateral triangle as below. Imagine that you are so far away from your spouse as both of you are distant from God as in the Figure below. If you determine to move closer to GOD as in the figure, you will immediately notice that the closer you are with God the closer you will become with your spouse; the distance between you and your wife will be shorter. You will always be pulled together as you become closer to God.

The Marriage Triangle— "A Threefold Cord is not Easily Broken"

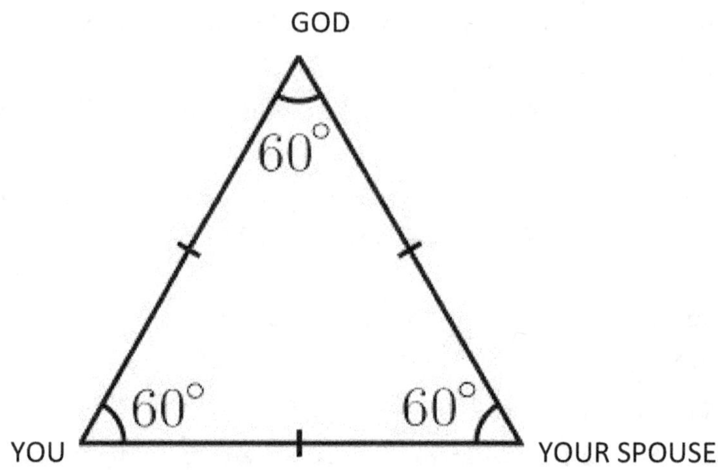

Remaining One in Marriage by keeping the Family Altar Fire burning. It must not die

In Leviticus 9 we read of the dedication of the Temple. When all the sacrifices have been made as instructed by Moses, Fire came from heaven in verse 24 and consumed the offering because the sacrifice had been accepted by God. In Leviticus 6:13, The Priests were instructed not to let the fire die. They must keep the fire burning on the Altar. The Priests must keep the fire burning, changing the logs and emptying the ashes. When Jesus came, the New Covenant came into being. The Physical Temple was no more. All believers have become the Temples of the Holy Spirit.

But we know that Jesus came to fulfill the Law not destroy it. In Acts chapter 1, it is recorded that Jesus had asked His Disciples to await The Promise of the Father – The Holy Spirit in Jerusalem as He was taken away before them to Heaven through the sky. As the disciples waited in Acts Chapter 2, at the appointed time, tongues of fire again came from heaven and landed on each of the disciples present and they were filled with The Holy Spirit. Acts 2:4

Remaining One in Marriage requires that the couple must not let the fire of the Holy Spirit die. The Fire must continue to burn. As a couple you must continue to stir up the gift of the Holy Spirit that came at Salvation and when you were joined together in Holy Matrimony. How do we keep the fire burning?

The first thing is **Praying together.** There is truth in this statement that **"the family which prays together stays together"**. The basis for this can be found in Matthew 18:19-20. "Again, I tell you truly that if two of you on the earth agree about anything you ask for, it will be done for you by My Father in heaven: *"For where two or three gather together in My name, there am I with them."*

Remember that Adam and Eve were together in the Garden of Eden. And God would come in the cool of the day to fellowship with them (Gen 3:8). So, the home starts with two who are now ONE as in the Book of Beginnings (Genesis). God was in their midst. So, as you and your wife pray together, God is constantly in your midst. And wherever the Spirit of God is, there is liberty i.e. freedom. 2 Corinthians 3:17, that is the freedom of children with their Father. Where He is there is Freedom, freedom from fear. Where the Spirit of God is there is illumination. Where the Spirit of God is there is sanctification.

Prayer keeps the Fire of the Holy Spirit burning. So, resolve to *"dwell in the secret place of the Most High"* so that you may *"abide under the shadow of the Almighty"*. (Psalm 91) That 'Secret place' is the Place of impregnable fortress, and a place of revelation. The invitation is to dwell there and not just visit on Sundays or now and then. Prayer is the way to dwell there. Apart from daily family prayer each must also have his or her own quiet time with the Lord also in prayer

Remaining One in marriage, requires that the Fire of The Holy Spirit must be kept burning through Family sharing of the Word in Home Bible Study Fellowship. Our goal, as disciples of Jesus Christ is to be like the Master. That was the goal for His first disciples. He called them *"that they might be with Him"* Mark 3:14. The disciples stayed with Him to observe Him that they might learn of Him and be able to do what he was doing and imitate Him. Before He departed to Heaven, He told His disciples in John 6:63, *"the words I speak to you, they are spirit and they are life."* The Bible is the Word of God. It is not a mere literature book to be studied and analyzed and the like. It is the Word of God to be believed and to be lived so that we might be like Christ.

I was once in counsel with a couple who were both Pastors. There were some issues going on between them and some of their children were in rebellion. During discussion I asked "what happens when you bring these matters to the altar during family prayer" and I discovered to my horror that they did not have home fellowship of prayer and study of the Bible together. No wonder, that was why they were covering themselves with *fig leaves*. The solution is the Family Altar of sharing the Word of God together so that our path may be lightened, (Psalm 119:105). We need to pray a prayer of repentance and recommitment where we do not have a family Bible Fellowship and prayer time.

A time of home Fellowship is also a time of family interaction, in an atmosphere of love. This is a time family member share together their experiences, their challenges and their needs especially while discussing the life application of shared Scripture. It is a time when members receive support from one another.

Recently I was on vacation in Australia with my daughter's family. My grandson, a nine-year-old shared during Bible Fellowship one evening concerning his fear of the attitude of a teacher to him who did not believe what he was saying even though he was telling the truth and tended to believe the other guy who was actually telling a lie. He did not want to have to face such an ordeal the next day. The sisters one 15 and the other 13 quickly offered counsel based on the Word of God and encouraged him. Then the family prayed for him specifically praying the Lord to intervene in the matter. And the Lord mercifully did this. The teacher never referred to the matter at all ever afterwards.

This was an incident that drew the children closer to God, knowing that they could bring any of their concerns to the Lord no matter how small or how great. The kids also experienced the power of unity in prayer and trust in God. I am sure we were all encouraged to gather for Bible Study at the Family Altar to learn and to share then Truth of the Word of God.

The Word is the Fulcrum of Oneness in Marriage

Jesus says in John 6:63, *"It is the spirit that quickeneth; the flesh profiteth nothing: the words that I speak unto you, they are spirit, and they are life."* If the words spoken by God are "spirit" and "life", then the Word of God, the Bible is the centrality of **remaining one** in marriage and should be embraced, tied to, every day for the oneness to remain stable. The Word is thus the Fulcrum of the Oneness of the Christian family, just like the oneness of the Holy Trinity. There is no one without the others in the Trinity. Husband and wife are complete as one only in Christ as they are held together in His Word by the power of the Holy Spirit.

Needless to say, marriage like our Christian Faith is all about Relationship as represented by the Cross. The Vertical of the Cross points to our relationship with God, while the Horizontal of the Cross points to our relationship with others. Without a close relationship with God, there can be no sustainable relationship with any other. As each, in a marriage becomes like Christ, each necessarily and progressively becomes like each other just as the disciples had become so like Christ that they were hardly distinguishable, which created the necessity for Jesus to be betrayed! Thus, it is the constant exposure to Jesus, "The Word" of God that transforms our lives to become more like Him.

The Theory of Attachment

There was a recent research study carried out by this author, between 2017 and 2018 among adolescents in a Christian middle School in Rustenburg, South Africa which "examined what effect if any, Bible Study Fellowship may have on the Relationship to God, of those who consistently participate in it, over time." The study arose out of the ongoing debate as to whether Sunday School Bible Study was still relevant in today's church, a question that has led to the decision of some churches to actually remove Sunday School from their Church programs.

The study was to test the *Theory of Attachment* in the realm of religion. This theory of attachment, developed by John Bowlby, a Psychologist, states that there is a bond between a child and its mother or caregiver, otherwise called an "Attachment Figure" (AF), that enables the child to feel secure when the caregiver is close by and insecure when the caregiver is not within reach or within sight.

It is that relationship that is called "attachment" and the essence of that relationship is proximity. The infant experiences "secure" attachment relationship when it finds that over time, it can count on the 'proximity' of the caregiver in time of danger. The infant becomes progressively secure that even when the caregiver is not within sight, it no longer frets because the infant has come to know that if there is danger the caregiver will be available. The infant attachment quality is insecure when from its experience it cannot count on the caregiver's availability in time of danger.

Accordingly, the quality of that attachment between a child and its caregiver, repeated and developed through daily experiences, serve as the model of all other social relationships throughout a person's life. It has implications for mental health and affects later life relationships such as the ability to develop and experience friendship as well as other interpersonal relationships including, marriage.

Now some core aspects of religious belief and behavior similar to the bond between a child and its caregiver are also evidenced in the Christian Faith. We are the children of God and our God is omnipresent, that is He is always in proximity. In time of danger, we know He is available and so we "cry" to Him. We even pray quietly to Him and meditate on His Word because we know that He is always available, always "by my side".

It is the exposure to and the understanding of the Word of God that promotes the bonding of the Christian "infant" to develop a bond/attachment to God. The Study in South Africa was to attempt to measure the effectiveness of the exposure of the learners in the Christian School to the Word of God in the development of a close relationship between the learners and God. The Word of God has the power to impart new life. A believer is *"born again"* through the *"living and enduring Word of God".*

This Truth that the Word of God has power to impart life is illustrated by the story of the appearance of Jesus to the two disciples who were on their way to the city of Emmaus in Luke 24:13-16. A disciple, Cleopas was walking with another disciple on Resurrection Day when they met Jesus. These disciples were probably running away from Jerusalem to avoid possible arrest by the authorities, of the followers of Jesus who had just been crucified that weekend.' They were totally dejected by the events of the previous few days which ended in the crucifixion of Jesus, a man *"powerful in word and deed"* whom they had hoped would be the one to *"to redeem Israel."*

Then at some point on the journey Jesus held a 'Bible Study Class' with them which consisted of explaining to them what was said in the Scriptures concerning Himself. He The Good Teacher that He is, took them to the Word showing them the story of Jesus as presented in the Bible. The hearing of the Word and the explanation of the Word transformed the lives of these two disciples. Before, they were running away from danger, now they were running back to Jerusalem the place of danger. So, these two disciples became closer to God even now that He was no longer physically around them; their bonding with Christ, their attachment to Jesus was now closer than before, because of the 'Bible Study'.

This theory was put to the test in the study of the adolescents in a Christian Middle School in South Africa to determine if the exposure of these students to the Word of God through Bible Study Fellowship for seven months would result in a closer relationship with God than those even though Christians in the same school but who were not so exposed. The findings in the study showed (1) that there was attachment relationship between the students and God that can be characterized as attachment to God and that (2) the level of the relationship, the quality of the bond was enhanced by the constant exposure to the Bible Study Fellowship. Therefore, this study shows that constant exposure to the Word of God makes us become closer to God.

Train up a Child in the Way He Should Go

Finally, my own personal experience in growing up in a family where constant Bible Fellowship and worship was mandatory, I can confirm the Word of God Proverbs 22: 6. *"Train up a child the way he should go; and when he grows up, he will not depart from it."* My parents had followed the mandate in Joshua 1:8: *"this Book of the Law must not depart from your mouth…"*

Does that mean that we would never stray? No. There is always a Prodigal in each of us. But since the indestructible seed is in there, the prodigal will come to himself and return home. The quality of the bond forged in our relationship with the Lord through our constant exposure to the Word in the study of the Word and in prayer will draw us back to God.

I strayed. Frustrated by the wickedness all around, and the prevalent hypocrisy of Christians in the world, one could go 'prodigal'. For instance, I dabbled into communism, believing at a time that the slogan of Communist Karl Marx: "From each according to His ability to each according to his needs", was actually the Gospel in practice as illustrated by the original Church in the Book of Acts 1: 44-45: *"And all that believed were together, and had all things common; And sold their possessions and goods, and parted them to all men, as every man had need."* But the Word brought me back.

"You Must be Doers of the Word and not only Hearers"

Remaining One in Marriage through holy living. 1 Peter 1:15. The Lord says *"Blessed are those who hear the Word of God and do it"*. (Luke 11:28). In Revelation 1:3, the Book of the Ending, the Word of God says Blessed is the one who reads aloud the words of this prophecy, and blessed are those who hear and obey what is written in it, because the time is near. In order to remain as One in Christ there must be holy living. Holy living is a life of love demonstrated in a life of obedience to God's Word. *"If you love me, you will obey my commandment."* And when, by the Grace of God, the children arrive in the home, they are going to be watching how the Word we read daily play out in their parents' lives and relationships with each other and with them.

What does it actually mean to live a holy life as a Christian and a couple? Being born again does not mean we are living a life of holiness?

It means living to please God in all your ways. You both have chosen to obey Him because you love him. How do you know you are living a holy life? The short and simple answer is James 4:4. *"Ye adulterers and adulteresses, know ye not that the friendship of the world is enmity with God? whosoever therefore will be a friend of the world is the enemy of God."* Therefore, to live a holy life, you need to disconnect with the world. In other words, do not be *"conformed to this world"* Romans 12:2. Does that mean you will never be tempted again? No. But a life dedicated to please God will flee from every appearance of evil. 1 Thessalonians 5:22. And if we keep to this, your spouse and the children cannot but experience it every day. With that they also become more like you and as you are becoming more and more like Christ, so also are becoming more and more like you.

Let me provide an example here as to how being a doer of the Word can resolve serious marriage situation. There was this couple who got married while they were both in the world. They met at a club and got married in a club surrounded by revelers like themselves. They hired three limousines for the event and really had a good time as good as it could be in this world system. The woman had had a child outside wedlock and did not know the father.

Let us call the couple John and Jane. Sometime later John became born again and his life literally changed as he became truly hungry for God. For some time, the wife played along pretending to have become born again as well. However, along the way she found that the life the husband was now living was totally different from what she knew and she could no longer pretend. For her, Sunday services were too long; church events were too frequent and she missed her parties, the type of lifestyle to which John had turned his back on. The new friends of the family were no longer satisfying. So, she devised to relocate and persuaded her husband to resign from his good job and move to another state, which he did. Although I had come into John's life and had agreed to disciple him, they had decided to relocate and had actually relocated before I got to know.

Soon in their new location, the wife resumed her club and party life and invited her mother down to live with them. By the time John let me know he was actually going through a lot of difficulty and thought the best thing was for him to file for divorce. First, he could not get a steady job for almost a year and there was no peace at home. Several times John would call me in the middle of the night to say that his wife just called him to come and pick her up in a party place; that she never told him where she was going nor with whom she was at the party. Then I would say to her, go and pick up your wife. This happened several times.

After some time, Jane found some reason to let her mother move into her bedroom when the husband was away from home briefly and from that time John had to move to the other bedroom. They had two girls together and the boy who was born before to another man before their marriage. Well, there were now more than sufficient grounds for him to get a divorce and each time I let him know, he could not do it and still be in obedience to the Word of God.

It turned out that Jane and a boyfriend she was having an affair with had planned to push John to seek a divorce so he could pay alimony and they could take over the house. Actually John had bought the house and only added his wife's name in deference to the Word of God that husband and wife are one in Christ. At that time John really feared for his life and called me that he had to get a divorce. One night around 2am John called me from the state in which they lived really sobbing and at the end of his patience. All along we have been praying together and seeking the guidance of God but determined to go by the Word of God and whatever He revealed for us to do in this matter.

So, when he called that day at 2 am and presented a scenario of what was happening, (I cannot remember what that was now), I myself was spellbound and did not know exactly how to explain what was in my mind which was that he should still not file a divorce but continue to seek the help of God to persevere. In answer to his question I simply asked him to go on 7 day fast, that I would join him in the fast and that I believe the Lord would strengthen him would speak to us. My constant counsel was that he could not divorce his wife under any circumstances but that in accordance with 1 Corinthians 7, verse 15, if the *"unbelieving spouse wishes to go, let him or her go"* but if not, then not because God hates divorce; He hates putting away, (Malachi 2: 16).

Soon after that I got a call from a friend of John's who informed that he had just seen John and that he was very thin and looking fragile. He suggested that his wife must have been giving him a really hard time and that the woman was not easy to live with. I immediately concluded that John must have been worrying whereas we were to trustingly leave this matter in God's hands. So, I called him and began to chide him for worrying, telling him his friend had just called me to say he looked worried.

And John said, "no I am not worried; you asked to fast for seven days." And I asked are you doing a continuous seven day dry fast, and he said Yes. Thereupon, I believed that there would be an answer soon. John was doing a desperate prayer and the Lord answers desperate prayers quickly like the Prayer of Jacob who wrestled with God. (Genesis 32:26)

A short while after the fast, his wife sued for divorce! In the court the Judge, a woman, was so impressed by the lengths John had gone in bending over backwards in the interest of his wife and children. She ordered that the two cars in the husband's name should be taken away from the wife and handed over to her husband. The property was to be sold when the youngest child reached the age of 18 and the proceeds shared as prescribed by the judgment. John again pleaded with the Judge to allow her to keep one of the cars for the sake of the children which the judge granted in admiration of the unusual large heart of john.

Since he became born again, John was popularly known as "Pastor" in his office. He organized a start the week with God ministry where people gathered early on Monday mornings at a local fast food place to share the Word of God together briefly and pray together. He was doing prison visits and was constantly on call by workmates who had any problem of any type because John was always ready to pray. When John returned to New York where he was before moving out to another state with his former wife, he went back to his old job to seek help for leads as to how to get a job. His old boss was still there and when he told him that he was back to New York and needed a job, his boss said: "Look, your old job is still there; the position had not been filled so you can take it back." Amazing grace. The Lord kept that desk waiting for John for two years and that was where he resumed work until he retired last year 2018. It pays to trust God and His Word and live a life of obedience to His Word.

Does this story mean we must submit to all kinds of abuse even if life threatening? No. But the answer is not divorce. There are so many options other than divorce and the Lord will always provide a way of escape to us if we are committed to a life of obedience to His Word.

Let me illustrate this need to obey God and trust His Word in another case in which I was involved in Nigeria, West Africa. I was working in an international organization and a friendly colleague who was the head of the Human Resources division came into my office early one morning and simply burst into tears. I shut the door and let her cry. She informed me that her husband came back home the previous night to say that a young lady gave birth to a baby for him and the mother of the young girl would accompany the young lady upon discharge from the hospital the following day until the naming ceremony was done on the seventh day. She said she was speechless and could not sleep overnight.

I asked what she wanted to do and she said she was totally beside herself, but she would not like to commit murder! They were married in England and her husband had said she did not want to have more than two children. And the two children were now grown up men and had left home. I let her know that I believed there had to be a reason he behaved as if your feelings did not count. If we hand over everything to The Lord, there is no heart he cannot touch; there is no problem He cannot solve. The only weapon that Satan cannot deal with is Love. Love never fails but only the Spirit of God can give us the strength to love the unlovable. It was sure that everybody was expecting a monumental fight. My counsel was to disarm them. The Word of God says *"Pursue peace."* The Law of Love requires it. Hebrew 12:14-15 and Romans 14:18-20

Now in Africa Baby naming ceremony was a very important and religious ceremony. So I advised and she followed the following advice:

On getting home she invited her husband to follow her to the local market to select the items normally used during traditional naming ceremony. They had extra rooms in the house. She prepared two rooms one for the mother of the young mother and one for the young mother and her baby. She decorated the two rooms very well and loaded the house with food. There was no argument, no questions asked and when the august guests arrived, they were warmly welcomed and ushered into their rooms. Whenever she felt overwhelmed with emotions and bitterness was going to creep in, she would go to the bathroom to go and cry on the neck of Jesus.

You see there is an interesting allegory in *Things Fall Apart* by Chinua Achebe about how mother hawk trained her little ones to carry out good hunting for food. Mother hawk would release the little ones to the 'earth' to go and bring a baby domestic bird on earth. First time the baby hawks swooped on the earth and captured two baby ducks. When they got home on top of the trees, the mother asked them what the mother duck did when they carried its babies. They said she did nothing; she just looked. The mother hawk told them to quickly return the birds and find another victim. They did that and then this time fought and captured two baby chicks. And when the same question was put to them, they reported that the mother hen was shouting and crying. Then mother Hawk said to its children, we can kill these ones and cook these ones and eat them because "there is nothing to fear from the one who shouts". (Proverbs 21:23; James 1:19). There is great wisdom in restraint when hurt. And when you have surrendered yourself totally to God, the Spirit of God is allowed to be in full control and you just leave things to Him. Jesus is our Advocate in heaven. Leave the case to Him.

So, the man came to his wife and confessed how under the influence of drink at a home party organized by his job there had been a moment of indiscretion with one of the ladies invited to entertain guests at the party. And when he was suddenly informed several months later that the lady was pregnant, he was at a loss what to do. His male friends had advised him to just bulldoze his way through the problem. And he followed their advice and found to his shock, that there was nothing to bulldoze and it was then he realized the depth of her love for him. So, by a most pleasant surprise there was repentance, there was forgiveness and the couple became closer to each other and to God more than ever before and they are still together to this day. Love conquers all 1 Peter 4:8

Children Raised in Christian Homes are Destined for Signs and Wonders

Remaining One in marriage requires keeping the Fire of the temple burning through a life of Faith. Without Faith we cannot please

God. And as families pray together, it has to be a prayer of Faith. (Hebrews 11:6). There is heartwarming story about a Christian Family in the University of Ife, Ile-Ife, Nigeria in the 1980s. The Fellowship in the Professor's Home Fellowship was so spiritually hot that believers in the University would refer a health emergency case to his house as a first step. This was very much before the days of cell phone and when even owning a normal phone was almost a status symbol. So emergency cases would be rushed to this Professor's house and the Lord was doing wonders through this Family Home Fellowship ministry.

One day there was an emergency. A child was suddenly very sick and the parents rushed the baby to the Professor's home. A young boy, the son of the Professor opened the door and the parents of the sick child rushed in and asked for his father. The young man said his father had traveled. The parents were immediately sad and alarmed. But the young man told them: "Do not worry, I will call on the Lord as my father does and everything will be okay". So, this young man laid his hand on the sick child and prayed a short prayer of healing on the child and the child was healed. God honored the prayer of the young boy, who was following the example of the parents in the prayer of faith. The fire on the family altar must be kept burning with prayer of faith daily. The Fire was already in this young boy because he was at the altar every day with his parents.

That also reminds me of one of my grandchildren in Atlanta, Eva Olaoluwa. I think she must have been about 6 years old at the time. We, grandparents had come visiting. And as we were about to depart, she looked a little downcast; so, I noticed that and invited her to pray. First, I was not sure she would actually do that; but I was ready to take up the prayer if she decided not to say anything. But she actually prayed in such a way that it was obvious that the Holy Spirit prayed through that kid. We all excited chorused Amen and no one needed to pray after that. The constant exposure of Eva to the Word of God through bedtime Bible reading and prayer had let her fall in love with the Lord in simple childlike faith.

She was being lighted up with the Fire of the family altar even as Samuel was doing at Eli's. The Fire must be kept burning with the wood of **Faith**. To keep the fire burning requires diligence on the part of the Priest. It is not when I feel like; you must be determined to keep the fire burning. In brief, to remain One in marriage, we must live the life of the Spirit. The Bible says in Galatians 5:24-26 that if we profess to live in the Spirit, then we must WALK in the Spirit, since we have crucified the flesh with its affections and lusts. A life in the Spirit is a life of Faith.

Let Me Also Testify as a PK (Preacher's Kid) of a Different Era

In concluding this section, I need to testify that, growing up I witnessed the power of the Spoken Word of God and the Power of Prayer of Faith at home. My father observed all the watches in prayer: 6am, 9am, 12midday, 3pm, 6pm and 9pm after which we all went to bed, unless when he was necessarily away from home or on the farm.

He was a Pastor and Church Planter and held street evangelism regularly. The Lord established through him, a Primary School which is today the largest Primary School in Ikere, in Ekiti State of Nigeria, our home town. The School is called God's Grace School while the Church that God founded through him was called God's Grace Church which is now called God's Grace Cathedral at the same location.

I witnessed many miracles growing up in our home. I am the oldest of 5 children 2 male 3 female. My father, Gabriel Omotoso, built a fairly big two floor house, with 6 bedrooms, 3 sitting rooms, but none of us had a permanent place to sleep. Our home was always filled with itinerary preachers or sick people being prayed for. I never liked it whenever I had to share his bed with him because he continued to observe the 3 hourly prayer times even at night!

There was only a small Dispensary in Ikere-Ekiti when I was growing up. There was no doctor, only a dispenser. There were only 11 telephone numbers in the town where I grew up and my father had one of them the types that you rolled their numbers clockwise to dial. The king of the town had one or two of them and the chiefs and perhaps local government officials in the town. Those who frequented our home did not have access to that facility: itinerary preachers, the sick in mind and the sick in body, the pregnant women who had problems with their pregnancy. But each time a sick person was going to be rushed to our home, The Holy Spirit let my father know ahead often during the Watch Hour home Fellowship prayer sessions. Then he would announce it at the end of the prayer session and we would all pray for this unknown individual who was going to be rushed to us

Women gave birth in our home routinely. Most of them were brought by their families because they were experiencing threatened abortions My father delivered the babies by praying the babies out of their mother's wombs and waiting to catch the babies. My mother was the nurse who assisted and washed the babies. Every child born in our home had an automatic given name. He was called "Gbadua" which literally means a child who survived by prayer.

I witnessed many manifestations of the power of God. On several occasions people brought cases to my father that he might settle some disagreement between them. Sometimes, as someone is trying to state his case, my father would stop him and say to the person. "The Holy Spirit is saying you are not telling the truth" and the fellow would break down and then state the truth. Later I read a similar manifestation of The Spirit in the episode recorded in Acts 5 about Ananias and Saphira.

Yes, our house was always full of people who have come for healing. And they got healed, some after a long time and some after a short time. The first thing my father did was to preach salvation to the patient. Once the person received salvation, he would assure them of God's healing. There were many women who came because they had difficulty getting pregnant. It's the same process: receive salvation and be coming to Church to hear the Word and to believe. And these women get pregnant and have their babies.

I could go on. But then I graduated from Primary School and went to a Christian Boarding School where I began to experience a more "civilized' form of Christianity. They read prayers from books. We had a hospital in the city where we received treatment if we were ill. We did not so much require Prayer for healing.

When I was very young, some sharp object pierced my skull in an accident. I was drenched with blood all over and rushed home. My father never panicked. He prayed; the blood stopped. He prayed on water, and washed the area. Every day he would dip a feather in olive oil on which he had prayed and drench the area with the olive oil covering the wound up with cotton wool. Any time the feather touched the area I felt the touch in my brain.

The scar is still on my head although the spot had shifted forward towards my forehead. When I got to the University and had to complete Student's medical registration form, I was asked if I ever suffered from head injury. I indicate 'Yes'. The doctor asked if I sometimes suffered from headaches or any other thing in my head and I said "No".

Reader, I am at pains to record my childhood experience here to provide for you, my personal experience as a witness to the Truth that marriage is not really about you but about the Kingdom of Heaven. It is to replenish the earth by bringing Godly seeds to the earth and ultimately to prepare you for heaven. It is to make you flourish and to enable you to obey the command to occupy until Jesus returns; Luke 19:11-27.

Your home should be church because The Lord has assured us that where two or three are gathered in His Name, He is there in their midst.

My prayer is that as you have read the above guidelines, you will surrender your life afresh to The Lord Jesus Christ. As you "gather together." If the Creator of The Universe is in your midst, if the God of Psalm 46 is in your midst, you would only be still and know that He is God. Amen

Some possible follow-up questions

Perhaps upon the completion of this reading at this point, you do have some lingering questions such as:

- I never had a father figure in my life to show me the way to go or, I never even knew my parents. No one was there for me to model for me what a happy home looked like. How can I fit into the model you are describing here?
- My Pastor has married and divorced two times; he is the third husband of his current wife, if my Pastor cannot satisfy this injunction, is it realistic for you to expect a higher standard from me?
- The whole world around me looks different from what you have featured in this Guideline. The culture of today says love is reciprocal. The morality of the world today gives you license to treat others the same way they treat you. So how can this ever work out within current culture?
- How is it possible to continue to be and live together **as one** with an abusive partner?

Conclusion

I am using this conclusion to address those concerns. The basis of the relationship presented in this Guideline is not the world's definition of love. The world's definition of love today is indeed reciprocal; it is called the Golden Rule. God's kind of love is different; the love that He wants His followers to show is the kind of love that is shown to the unlovable the type that Jesus showed to us while we were yet His enemy; the type that was praying for us while we were nailing Him to the Cross; the type that never insisted on His Rights nor used His Power to pay us back what we deserved.

Yes, you will easily say 'Yes, but He was God and I am human'. Yes, He was God but He was also hundred percent human. Remember that at the Garden of Gethsemane, angels needed to come and strengthen Him, because He was experiencing pain as a human, so also on the Cross and the grueling journey to the Cross. If like Him, we think, move, and do only what we see our Lord do in His Word, if we live according to His Word, His Holy Spirit inside us will then lead us into all Truth in any situation or circumstance. I have not heard of any one or read of any account of anyone who put His total trust in God in any matter, and who was then put to shame on the matter. Psalm 69:6;

Psalm 125:1-2

This Guideline is addressed primarily to those who are committed disciples of Jesus Christ and who therefore have the Holy Spirit residing in them. These ones know who they are and whose they are. But the Guideline is not addressed exclusively to them. It is addressed to all who wish to know or who want to renew their identity in Christ. It does not matter how long you have been away from home or have deviated from the path. Jesus, the Father of the Prodigal son, is always waiting for us. Once you discover or recover your identity by being "born again" and committed to follow Christ, you now have a Father who NEVER deserts and Who is ALWAYS a prayer away. In order to recover all the enemy has stolen from you, come to the Father today through Jesus Christ and everything the enemy has stolen from you, you will recover and with increase. In the Kingdom you now belong to, you will be enabled by the Power of the Holy Spirit to follow the Word of God, and to live the Word not as the world lives by in Philosophy and dictates of man. When you taste you will see *"how gracious The Lord is…"* (Psalm 34:8).

In the Kingdom to which we now belong as members of the Royal Priesthood, we are required to love the kind of people that we would have a hard time loving. Included in this group would be our difficult

Spouses, who "cheat on us". It is the kind of love expressed in Matthew 5:46-48. Actually, cheating on you is a minor problem. They are "cheating on God" from whom nothing is actually hidden. So, the cheating spouse needs intercessory prayer. To rage and devour one another is to say that God really has nothing to do or say on the issue.

But are we ever able to do this? Certainly not. Okay this is problematic. The Lord requires us to do this and yet it is impossible for us to meet this standard. Paul was in this dilemma too. *'The good that I want to do I cannot do and the evil that I do not want to do, that is what I do.'* He then cried for deliverance and found the solution Romans 7: 15-25. So, the Pastor is not our model; we are fellow travelers with him only as far as he follows Christ. Our focus is not on him but on Jesus Christ.

Andrew A. Omotoso

We can never do this in our own strength. It is not a question of will power. We are the called-out ones and a call to salvation is actually a call to come and die. The flesh must die, and die daily (1 Corinthians 15: 31.) Marriage is not just about here and now, it is about the Kingdom. It is to prepare you on your journey to heaven. There is nothing The Lord asks to do that we cannot do. He is not a liar. But there is none of them we can do without the Holy Spirit. And the Holy Spirit is available to all who believe and who all who ask for His help. That is the Key to the position on which this guideline rests. In my forty-seven plus year of marriage, I can testify that it gets sweeter every day simply on account of the Principles of the Kingdom portrayed in this piece of testimony.

Finally, you might say, I messed up my opportunity already. I am on my second marriage. I wish I had known this before. God is always giving us another chance. The chance starts with repentance and commitment to do things God's way from now on. He is a miracle worker.

He will restore you if you let Him and if you learn to trust Him.

www.ingramcontent.com/pod-product-compliance
Lightning Source LLC
Chambersburg PA
CBHW051449150726
48000CB00005B/2322